...னாதிபதியின் சுதந்திர தின உரையில் ...குடியேற்ற செய்தி இடம்பெற வேண்டும்

...மலையில் சுதந்திரதினம் நடந்ததற்கான மகிழ்வு ஏற்படும் என்கிறார் நாகேஸ்வரன்

எச்.ஐ.வி.தாக்கத்திற்குள்ளானோ... இனங்காணப்படுவதாக அமைச்சு ...

Hidden Kitchens of
Sri Lanka

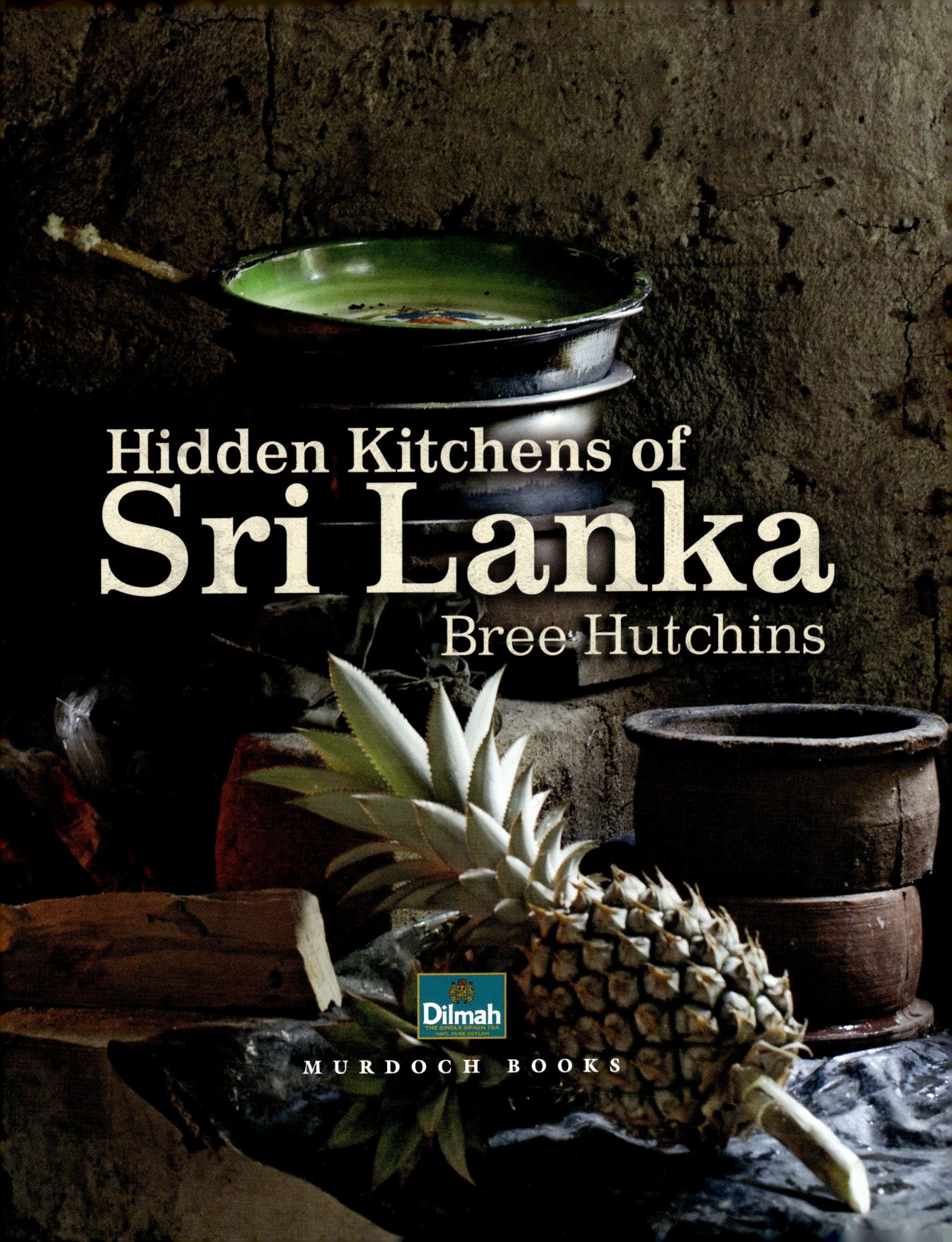

Hidden Kitchens of
Sri Lanka
Bree Hutchins

MURDOCH BOOKS

CONTENTS

THE JOURNEY BEGINS

I am heading down a narrow sandy path in Valvettithurai on the Jaffna Peninsula. It's late January 2012, the sun is blistering hot and not a breath of wind is coming off the Indian Ocean. The colourful wooden fishing boats and sunburnt palmyra palms are completely still. My companions — another photographer and a film crew — struggle in the heat, but our Sri Lankan guide doesn't seem to notice the sweat that streams down his back.

I've been in Sri Lanka for a month, documenting the work of the MJF Charitable Foundation, which was established in 1962 by Merrill J Fernando, the founder of Dilmah. In two weeks I'm due to fly home to Sydney, but I'm not ready to leave. It's not just that this tiny tropical island is stunningly beautiful and barely touched by tourism, it's also the people I have met; I am captivated by them. They have endured so much through three decades of civil war and the devastating 2004 tsunami, yet they possess a resilience, determination and positivity that I find awe inspiring. They don't just welcome strangers with a smile, they invite them into their homes to share a meal or a cup of tea with their families. Their hospitality is genuine and heartfelt. And … they are incredible cooks.

As we stop to take a few photographs, I turn to our guide, who is also the marketing manager of Dilmah, and surprise myself when I blurt out, 'Wouldn't it be incredible to travel around the country and stay with local families, to hear their stories and learn their family recipes?' I'm even more surprised when he replies, 'Why don't you? You could write a book and take the photographs. Dilmah could sponsor the publication.' And, as serendipitously as that, I land my first book deal on a sandy pathway on the Jaffna Peninsula.

With my heart still in Sri Lanka, I fly back briefly to Sydney to map out a plan for the book and find an editor and designer. I recognise that the journey on which I'm about to embark will be challenging and stretch me to my limits, but I also know it will be incredibly rewarding.

————————— ✳ —————————

I returned to Sri Lanka in time for Sinhalese and Tamil New Year. Over the next few months I explored the hidden kitchens of Colombo, ventured deep into the remote rural villages of the East, cooked with the inmates of Monaragala Prison and stayed at an army camp in Vakarai. I travelled north to the Jaffna Peninsula, my

favourite place in Sri Lanka, where I was caught up in a flurry of saris and chariots at a Hindu temple festival, and was spoilt rotten by two war widows.

My enthusiasm to photograph everything created much entertainment for the locals. When I wasn't wandering into people's kitchens, lured by spicy aromas, I was clambering up ladders and over fences, wading fully clothed into water or perching on stacks of rickety crates in busy market places — all for the perfect shot.

While my travels took me all around Sri Lanka, I spent most of my time in the East and the North, which until recently has been inaccessible because of civil war. With the help of Dilmah and the MJF Charitable Foundation, I was able to visit places not many foreigners have been allowed to enter. While tensions still exist in some areas, I never felt unsafe. Many towns are scarred by the war and the tsunami and there are a multitude of aid agencies working hard to repair the devastation. I was able to see first-hand the impact that assistance from charities such as the MJF Foundation has on people's lives. While the Fernando family is very humble about the work of the Foundation, from what I saw it is playing a vital role in the country's recovery.

This book is a collection of stories and recipes given to me by the people I connected with on my travels, many of whom I met by chance in market places or at roadside stalls. It didn't matter whether they were Buddhist or Hindu, Muslim or Christian, rich or poor, I was accepted without question and they openly shared their recipes, homes and histories with me. Listening to their stories would sometimes be heartbreaking and haunting, but they were always inspiring and full of promise.

Food plays a pivotal role in Sri Lankan culture and is used to celebrate festivals, religious ceremonies and every major event in a person's life. Sri Lankans are incredibly proud of their cuisine and cook from recipes handed down orally from one generation to the next. They don't measure ingredients, instead adding a handful of this and a pinch of that, according to intuition and taste. This made it rather challenging to estimate the quantities as I scribbled down recipes, however I was very fortunate to have my Sri Lankan friend Neyome with me. Neyome speaks Sinhala and Tamil and endeavoured to translate the cooking methods and explain some of the unusual ingredients. Each recipe is one person's version of a dish and I have tried not to alter it, except where the ingredients may be unobtainable or the traditional cooking methods too laborious.

Back home in Sydney I love cooking these recipes. And each time I do, I am transported back to a dimly lit kitchen in a mud hut, or a roadside stall, or to a home hidden away in a rural village, and reminded of tales told while we prepared fragrant curries, spicy fried snacks and rich sweets together. I hope you will also enjoy cooking these recipes and reading the stories of those who shared a small part of their lives with me.

THE WEST
Colombo

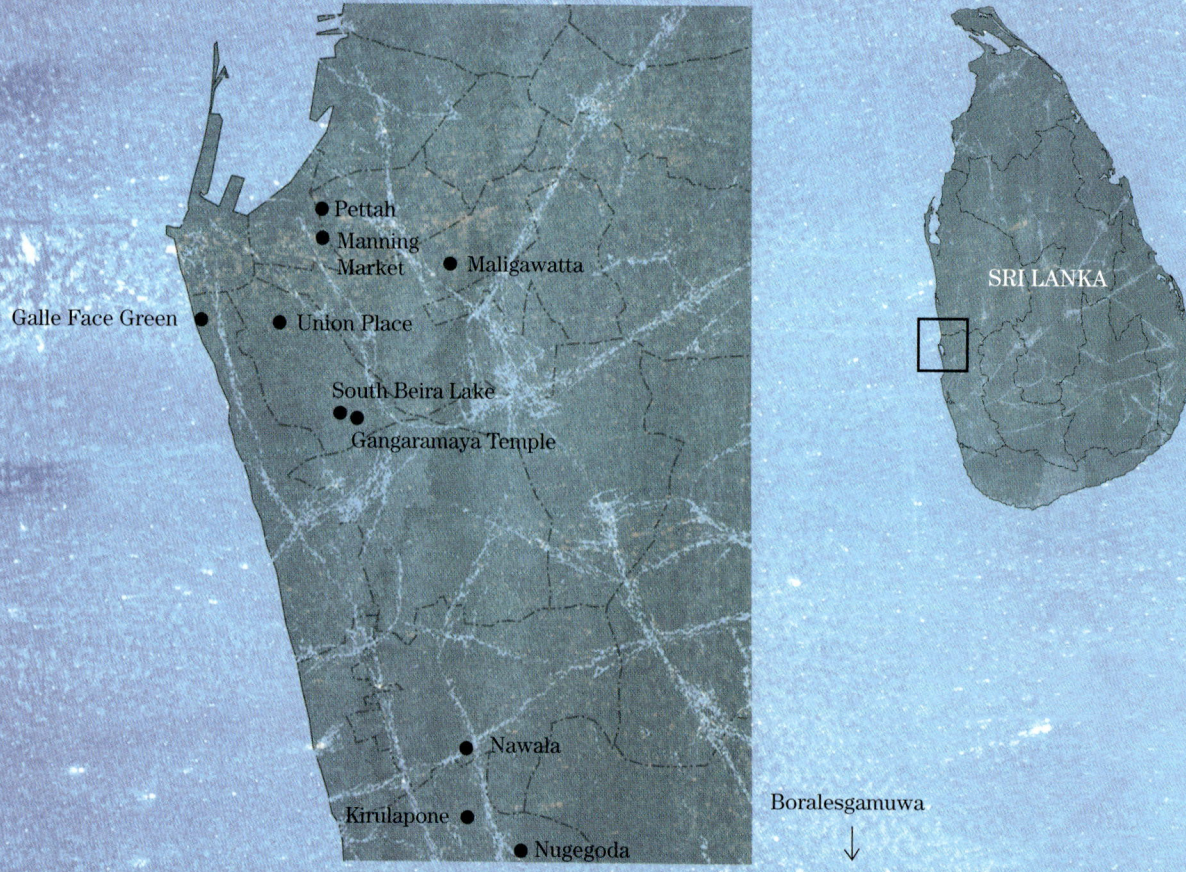

Pettah
Manning Market
Maligawatta
Galle Face Green
Union Place
South Beira Lake
Gangaramaya Temple
SRI LANKA
Nawala
Kirulapone
Nugegoda
Boralesgamuwa
↓

Sri Lanka's capital and ethnic melting pot, Colombo is a jumble of Buddhist and Hindu temples, mosques and churches. The city is changing fast, but is skilfully maintaining its sense of identity. Old Colonial buildings and sprawling markets sit amid towering skyscrapers, gleaming shopping malls, pumping nightclubs and trendy bars. Colombo is alive with a sense that 'it's the place to be'.

Taking a tuk-tuk and exploring the neighbourhoods less frequented by tourists gives an insight into how the city ticks. Colombo offers some of the country's most culturally diverse food. To sample some, head down to Galle Face Green, the best place for Sri Lankan street food.

PETTAH MANNING MARKET
William

It is almost 3 am and Pettah, Colombo's busiest and most hectic shopping district, looks uncharacteristically calm. There isn't a stallholder in sight flogging a sari, gold necklace or mobile phone.

But just north of the railway station, off Olcott Mawatha, momentum is starting to build. Colourful lorries, overloaded with bananas, pineapples and mangoes, are fighting to squeeze into the narrow laneways that will soon be congested to biblical proportions. Hunched coolies struggle with loads triple their weight, grunting '*jer*, *jer*' to warn anyone in their path. This is the first glimpse of what will soon be the chaos and life of Pettah Manning Wholesale Market.

Tucked away on a small patch of spare footpath is a bony, weathered man called William, crouching over a small fire, boiling water to brew his first pot of tea. His day is well underway; he has already travelled one and a half hours by bus from his home in Hanwella. Today has the same rhythm for William as every day for the last sixty-odd years.

A hot cup of William's milky tea is a treat for many at this early hour, and a chance to rest weary bodies on sacks of vegetables and dangle aching legs off lorries.

When trading officially commences at 5 am, the laneways are already a colourful blur of commerce and chaos. The only safe way to dodge the coolies weaving in and out at hypersonic speed is to clamber up on one of the many fruit crates. And it's from this vantage point that you get to experience the full sensory onslaught with all its noise, dirt and heat.

Darting through the crowds, tray in hand, is William, delivering tea. Everyone is too frantic to exchange greetings or money until the morning sale frenzy ends. Then William returns for a chat and to collect his 20 rupees.

By 8 am, when most tourists are waking up in shiny hotel rooms across Colombo, William is stretched out on a wooden crate, sipping a well-earned cup of tea. If he isn't chased off by council officers, he has time to wash the tea glasses and pack up his stall before he boards the bus. He'll go to bed soon after arriving home, only to get up at midnight to do this all again.

SPICY CEYLON TEA

Serves 4

Even though William's tea is only a simple blend of powdered milk and strong black tea, it is very popular among the stallholders and coolies. I was inspired by his tea to create this recipe, using spices that are sold at the markets and grown locally in Sri Lanka.

INGREDIENTS

12 green cardamom pods

12 black peppercorns

6 cloves

1 teaspoon fennel seeds

1 cinnamon stick, broken in half

3 cm (1¼ inch) piece ginger, roughly sliced

500 ml (17 fl oz/2 cups) full-cream milk

1 tablespoon jaggery powder*

1 tablespoon Dilmah Pure Ceylon tea leaves (or any other full-bodied black tea)

METHOD

Using a mortar and pestle, pound the cardamom pods, peppercorns, cloves, fennel seeds, cinnamon stick and ginger into a coarse paste.

Put the pounded spices and the milk into a small saucepan and place over medium heat. Stir in the jaggery and bring to the boil. When the milk reaches boiling point, immediately remove from the heat and gently stir in the tea leaves. Cover and infuse for 5 minutes.

Pour the tea through a small sieve into a jug. To create a froth, pour the tea into four small glasses from a height (about 30 cm/12 inches). Serve with kokis (page 100).

GALLE FACE GREEN
Rahuft

Rahuft stands behind his cart, chatting and laughing as he dishes up another plate of *isso vadai* (fried lentil patties topped with prawns). Soon it will be dark and in a few hours' time, around midnight, Rahuft will pack away his stall and push his cart back home, past the empty restaurants, glitzy nightclubs and sleeping skyscrapers. Then go up to his tiny room, hang his shirt on a rope strung to the wall, and move woks, trays and bottles of oil to one side to clear a space to sleep.

Rahuft is one of many food vendors down at Galle Face Green, a long stretch of grass and promenade that faces the Indian Ocean. Coming from a family of twelve, he is completely unfazed by the hordes of people who pour in at sunset to enjoy the open space. Working alongside his uncle Rasheed in the family business seven days a week, Rahuft doesn't get much time to do the things most young men do, but on a night like tonight when people are queuing up at his stall waving 50 rupee notes in their hands, he wouldn't want to be anywhere else.

It's a Saturday and the grass is dotted with families picnicking, vendors selling toys, and people flying kites and playing games. The promenade is lined with food carts selling mangoes dusted in chilli and salt; chickpeas tossed in grated coconut and chilli (*kadala*); diced *roti* fried with meat and vegetables (*kottu roti*); and the specialty among the vendors, *isso vadai*. Down at the water's edge, swarms of people chase waves and soccer balls, and up on the pier, people cram in to catch a glimpse of the setting sun. All this is taking place to a soundtrack of sizzling oil, the tak-a-tak of metal blades dicing *kottu roti*, the tinkling bells of vendors selling wads of spiced coconut wrapped in betel leaves, and the tooting horns of ice-cream vendors.

Earlier today, down a small laneway off a busy street on Union Place, I watched Rahuft and his uncle prepare for tonight. As always, the whole family was there to lend a hand. In the downstairs room, his cousins shaped a mixture of flour, coconut and chana dhal into balls. Outside, his brother washed the prawns at the communal tap. Upstairs, in a space that doubles as the bedroom, Rahuft and his younger sister pressed prawns into balls of mixture and flattened them into discs. These were passed to their uncle, who plunged them into vats of spitting oil, which sent a distinct, almost pungent, aroma through the tiny window and out into the laneway.

Rahuft's mother, in her hijab, travelled up and down the stairs, swapping buckets of mixture for trays of fried *vadai*. When there wasn't an unfried *vadai* in sight, Rahuft and his uncle carried the trays outside to load up their carts. They then set off down the street, Rahuft pushing his yellow cart and his uncle pushing his green cart out into the blurring traffic.

21

PRAWN VADAI

Makes about 15

Isso (prawn) vadai, a popular snack or 'short eat' at Galle Face Green, are crisp, deep-fried lentil patties topped with small prawns, and doused with a tangy chilli sauce. Munching on a plate of these while the sun sets over the Indian Ocean certainly beats any five-star-restaurant experience. Many stalls sell prawn vadai; one popular with the locals is run by Rahuft and his uncle. This is their recipe.

INGREDIENTS

200 g (7 oz/1 cup) chana dhal*, soaked in water for 4 hours

60 g (2¼ oz/½ cup) freshly scraped coconut*

small pinch of egg yellow powdered food colouring*, dissolved in 1 tablespoon water

50 g (1¾ oz/⅓ cup) plain flour, plus extra for dusting

2 teaspoons salt

60 small green (raw) school prawns (about 300 g/10½ oz), unpeeled, washed

vegetable oil, for deep-frying

200 g (7 oz) cabbage, very finely shredded

½ red onion*, very thinly sliced

1 carrot, very thinly sliced into 4 cm (1½ inch) strips

1 long, yellow banana chilli, very thinly sliced into 4 cm (1½ inch) strips

juice of ½ lime

METHOD

Drain the soaked dhal, then rinse and drain again; set aside 120 g (4¼ oz/¾ cup) of the soaked dhal. Process the rest of the dhal in a food processor to make a fine paste (do not add any water).

In a large bowl, combine the coconut with the dissolved food colouring. Wearing gloves, mix well with your hands to combine. Add the processed dhal and whole dhal and mix well. Sift in the flour and salt; mix with your hands to form a sticky dough. Take a small handful of the dough (about 30 g/1 oz) and work it into a ball the size of a walnut. Repeat to make 15 balls.

Take a ball of dough and place it between two pieces of plastic wrap, and place on a hard surface. Using the palm of your hand, press down to slightly flatten the ball. Remove the top piece of plastic and arrange 4 prawns on the dough ball, placing them in a straight row and all facing the same direction. Place the piece of plastic on top, then use your palm to press down hard to flatten the discs until they are about 7 cm (2¾ inches) in diameter and 4 mm (⅛ inch) thick. Remove both pieces of plastic wrap and dust the top and bottom of the discs with a little flour.

Fill a large wok one-third full of oil and heat to approximately 160°C (315°F) (a cube of bread dropped into the oil will brown in 30 seconds). Fry in batches for 2–3 minutes, or until golden brown. Remove with a slotted spoon and drain on paper towel. Meanwhile, combine the cabbage, onion, carrot, chilli and lime juice in a bowl; toss well. Serve the prawn vadai warm with chilli sauce (page 26) and the cabbage salad.

CHILLI SAUCE

Makes 500 ml (17 fl oz/2 cups)

This hot, tangy chilli sauce is the ultimate condiment to have with prawn vadai. Rahuft and his uncle make a batch once a week and when I visited they had already made the week's supply, but Rahuft was kind enough to share the recipe with me. He didn't know the precise quantities for each ingredient and the cooking method was a little vague, so this is more of an inspired version of their recipe.

INGREDIENTS

8 cm (3¼ inch) piece lemongrass, white part only, very finely chopped

4 cloves garlic, thinly sliced

3 cm (1¼ inch) piece ginger, thinly sliced

2 teaspoons salt

2 tablespoons vegetable oil

8 cm (3¼ inch) piece rampe (pandanus) leaf*

1 teaspoon cumin seeds

1 teaspoon mustard seeds

½ teaspoon fenugreek seeds

1 cinnamon stick

1 teaspoon unroasted chilli powder*

1½ teaspoons roasted curry powder (store-bought)

1 teaspoon ground turmeric

1 teaspoon ground coriander

1½ tablespoons coconut vinegar* (or rice vinegar)

1 tablespoon tomato ketchup

300 g (10½ oz) tinned tomatoes, puréed

METHOD

Using a mortar and pestle, pound the lemongrass, garlic, ginger and salt into a paste. Heat the oil in a saucepan over low–medium heat and fry the paste with the rampe, cumin and mustard seeds for 3 minutes, stirring regularly so the paste doesn't stick to the bottom of the pan.

Add the fenugreek seeds, cinnamon stick, chilli powder, curry powder, turmeric and coriander and cook for 1 minute. Add the coconut vinegar and 250 ml (9 fl oz/1 cup) water and bring to the boil, then reduce the heat to low–medium and simmer for 10 minutes.

Remove from the heat and strain through a fine sieve into another saucepan, discarding the solids. Return the liquid to the stove, and add the tomato ketchup and tomatoes. Bring to the boil, then simmer over low–medium heat for 15 minutes, or until the sauce has thickened. Allow to cool to room temperature before serving.

MUSLIM FAMILY FEAST

Faakhir & Fareena

Watching eighteen-year-old Faakhir scribble chemistry formulas with ease on a whiteboard in front of a classroom of young students, I'm not surprised when he confidently tells me, 'I want to be a doctor, *inshallah*.'

Five years ago Faakhir's story was very different. He thought he was destined to be like all the other kids on the street. Born into a poor family who live in the crowded Maligawatta slums, he never imagined that his life could be any different and he certainly never dreamt of applying to medical school.

His mother Fareena, however, wanted something more for him. She had heard from other mothers in the slum about the MJF Kids Programme, where children from the slums are given the chance to study and learn new skills. When she encouraged Faakhir to apply, he initially refused. Like many of the other kids living in the slums, Faakhir grew up not knowing his own capabilities.

As time passed, Faakhir began to notice something different in the children who participated in the MJF Kids Programme. It wasn't just the way they began to hold their heads higher, or how they strode with longer steps, but their whole energy changed and they started radiating a sense of possibility. Lured by what he saw in these children and with his mother's unwavering encouragement, Faakhir enrolled in the programme.

The classes were held after school each day and also on Saturdays, at the offices of the MJF Group (Dilmah), not far from the slums. Faakhir thought it was rather bizarre going to classes in the same premises as businessmen in suits, but he loved the programme and soon discovered there were things he was good at, such as science, public speaking and music.

At the same time that Faakhir was rewriting his destiny, so too was his mother. Fareena would wait while her son attended his classes, offering support to the young girls she met there, and volunteering to cook when there was a special event. Her sister Razeena also helped out, as her son also participated in the programme. They became surrogate mothers to all the children and were soon offered positions as volunteer Programme Coordinators. Working outside the family home was a break from her traditional cultural role, but Fareena's husband encouraged her to accept the position.

———————— ✳ ————————

Faakhir has now graduated from the MJF Kids Programme and teaches science to the younger students, as a way of giving back to the community, while he studies for his final high school examinations. Fareena smiles broadly when she tells me, 'The change in Faakhir has been profound. He has realised his potential and I thank Allah every day for this gift.'

Today Fareena and her sister have been busy cooking since 4 am. It's a tradition in their family to get together on Fridays and enjoy a big lunch after the midday prayer, the most important Muslim prayer of the week. I feel privileged to have been invited to join them.

'We are staying with my sister for a while,' Fareena explains. 'Our house was flooded during the heavy monsoon rains a few weeks ago.' This must be a welcome change for Fareena; her sister's house is really quite comfortable in comparison to her own home in the slums.

'We always make *biryani* on Fridays, either with chicken or mutton,' she says. 'We make lots of curries, pickles and salads to go with the *biryani*, too. Oh, and of course dessert,' she assures me, whisking more sugar into the mixture for the *vattalappam*, a coconut custard pudding.

Once the *vattalappam* has been placed in the double steamer on the stove, Fareena picks up a tray of marinated chickens and I follow her outside, where she has set up a gas burner and a large wok. We chat with ease as she fries the chickens, rhythmically spooning hot oil over them.

'Today Fareena and her sister have been busy cooking since 4 am. It's a tradition in their family to get together on Fridays and enjoy a big lunch after the midday prayer …'

We take a short break from cooking and Fareena pours everyone a glass of *faluda*, a pink drink made from rose sherbet syrup, milk, basil seeds, vermicelli noodles and red jelly. The drink is delicious and refreshing on such a hot morning.

It's time to layer the *biryani* and Fareena begins by filling a big pot with rice and chicken korma curry, which she mixes together. She places a layer of rice on top, and sprinkles over cashews and raisins that have been fried in ghee. She garnishes it with caramelised onions, spices and fresh coriander, then drizzles over some rosewater. The *biryani* looks impressive and smells sensational.

Fareena sets out all the dishes on a rug on the lounge-room floor. When Faakhir and his father return from the mosque, and his two younger sisters return from school, Fareena spoons the *biryani* onto a large circular communal dish, called a *sawan*. We sit in a circle around the dish and chat happily as we scoop up handfuls of *biryani* with our right hands. The flavours are incredible and I have to remember to pace myself so I can leave room for dessert.

CHICKEN BIRYANI

Serves 8

A meal of layered rice and curry, biryani is a popular Muslim dish all over the world. In Sri Lanka it is served with a mind-boggling array of accompanying curries, pickles and salads. Biryani is often steamed or baked, however Fareena didn't do this and I have to admit my first thought was 'it's not biryani!' But once I tasted it, I couldn't have cared less whether it had been steamed or not — it was absolutely sensational. Making biryani takes the best part of a day, but it's worth the effort. It's one of those dishes that needs to be shared and is great when served on a communal platter.

INGREDIENTS

biryani chicken korma curry (page 35)

biryani garnish no. 1 (page 38)

biryani garnish no. 2 (page 39)

2 teaspoons ground turmeric

60 ml (2 fl oz/¼ cup) vegetable oil

600 g (1 lb 5 oz/3 cups) basmati
  rice, washed

1 teaspoon salt

1 tablespoon ghee

80 g (2¾ oz/½ cup) raw cashew nuts,
  roughly chopped

50 g (1¾ oz/⅓ cup) raisins

3 teaspoons rosewater

METHOD

Prepare the chicken korma curry and the two biryani garnishes.

Place the turmeric and oil in a large saucepan and cook over low heat for 1 minute. Stir in the rice and salt, then add enough water to cover the rice by about 2 cm (¾ inch). Cover and bring to the boil, then reduce the heat to low and simmer for 20 minutes, or until the rice is cooked.

Heat the ghee in a small frying pan over low heat. Add the cashews and raisins and fry for 2–3 minutes, or until golden brown. Drain and set aside.

Transfer half of the cooked rice to a large, round pot or dish (about 8 litre (280 fl oz/32 cup) capacity and 26 cm (10½ inch) diameter) and mix with the chicken korma curry. Place the rest of the rice on top, but do not mix it with the bottom layer. Sprinkle garnish no. 1 on top and then garnish with the fried cashews and raisins. Drizzle the rosewater over the top.

Serve on a large shallow platter with garnish no. 2 on the side. For a complete Sri Lankan Muslim feast, also serve with fried whole chicken with spicy sauce (page 40) and green gram curry (page 46).

BIRYANI CHICKEN KORMA CURRY

Serves 8

This is a mild, aromatic tomato-based chicken and potato curry. It is mixed with rice to form the bottom layer of the biryani. *This curry is also delicious on its own with fragrant samba rice (page 49).*

INGREDIENTS

1 kg (2 lb 4 oz) all-purpose
    potatoes, unpeeled

1.6 kg (3 lb 8 oz) whole chicken

1 tablespoon vegetable oil

2 red onions*, sliced

10 cm (4 inch) piece rampe (pandanus)
    leaf*, cut into 2 cm (¾ inch) pieces

2 sprigs curry leaves, leaves picked

6 cm (2½ inch) piece lemongrass, white
    part only, finely chopped

2 cinnamon sticks, broken into pieces

6 cloves

6 green cardamom pods, bruised

3 cloves garlic, ground into a paste

4 cm (1½ inch) piece ginger, ground
    into a paste

8 roma tomatoes, cut into quarters

2 teaspoons salt, dissolved in 60 ml
    (2 fl oz/¼ cup) warm water

1 small chicken stock cube, dissolved in
    375 ml (13 fl oz/1½ cups) boiling water

4 tablespoons korma spice mix
    (store-bought)

1 tablespoon roasted chilli powder*

1 teaspoon freshly ground black pepper

1 teaspoon ground cumin

125 ml (4 fl oz/½ cup) soy sauce

60 ml (2 fl oz/¼ cup) tomato purée

METHOD

Boil the whole potatoes in a large saucepan until tender, then drain. When cool, peel and cut into 3–4 cm (1¼–1½ inch) pieces.

Place the chicken on a chopping board. Using a large knife or poultry scissors, joint the chicken into 8 pieces. Then, using a cleaver or large, heavy kitchen knife, cut the chicken through the bone into 4–5 cm (1½–2 inch) pieces. Place the chicken pieces in a bowl and set aside.

Heat the oil in a large heavy-based saucepan over medium heat, then add the onions, rampe, curry leaves, lemongrass, cinnamon sticks, cloves and cardamom pods; cook for 5 minutes, or until the onions are golden brown. Add the garlic paste and ginger paste and cook for a further 2 minutes. Add the tomatoes, salty water and stock, cover and bring to the boil.

Add the chicken pieces, korma spice mix, chilli powder, pepper and cumin and mix to combine. Stir in the soy sauce and tomato purée. The chicken pieces should be almost covered in liquid — if needed, add a little water. Cover and cook for 10 minutes, then remove the lid and cook for a further 30 minutes, or until the chicken is cooked and the sauce has thickened and reduced slightly. Stir in the boiled potato. Set aside until the rice for the biryani is ready.

35

BIRYANI GARNISH NO. 1

This garnish is sprinkled on the top layer of the biryani before it is served. It adds a wonderful rich depth of flavour and it's what makes the biryani so ridiculously delicious. There is an alarming amount of butter, but trust me, it works! The onions are basically shallow-fried in the butter, which is infused with lemongrass, curry leaves, cinnamon and spices. It's decadent but frighteningly good.

INGREDIENTS

2 tablespoons ghee

100 g (3½ oz/⅔ cup) raw cashew nuts, roughly chopped

250 g (9 oz) unsalted butter

2 red onions*, thinly sliced

2–3 long green chillies*, sliced

10 cm (4 inch) piece rampe (pandanus) leaf*, cut into 1 cm (½ inch) pieces

2 sprigs curry leaves, leaves picked and torn

6 cm (2½ inch) piece lemongrass, white part only, very finely chopped

5 cloves garlic, ground into a paste

5 cm (2 inch) piece ginger, ground into a paste

2 cinnamon sticks, broken in half

50 g (1¾ oz/⅓ cup) raisins

20 g (¾ oz/½ cup) finely chopped coriander leaves

20 g (¾ oz/½ cup) finely chopped mint

METHOD

Melt the ghee in a large heavy-based frying pan over medium heat. Add the cashews and cook for 2 minutes, stirring regularly until golden. Remove the cashews with a slotted spoon and set aside. Melt the butter in the frying pan, then add the onions, chillies, rampe, curry leaves and lemongrass. Cook over medium heat for 5–7 minutes, stirring regularly, until the onions are light golden.

Add the garlic paste, ginger paste and cinnamon sticks and stir well; cook for a further 4–5 minutes, or until the onions are dark golden. Stir in the cashews, raisins, coriander and mint, then remove from the heat and set aside.

BIRYANI GARNISH NO. 2

This garnish is served as a side dish and sprinkled on top of the biryani by the head of the family. It adds a crisp texture to the biryani and a typical salty–sour Sri Lankan flavour from the Maldive fish and lemon. The flavours and textures contrast perfectly with the caramelised onion garnish and help to balance its buttery richness.

INGREDIENTS

80 ml (2½ fl oz/⅓ cup) coconut oil*

2 red onions*, very thinly sliced

1 teaspoon Maldive fish pieces*
   (preferably flakes)

½ teaspoon dried chilli pieces*

1 teaspoon lemon juice

pinch of salt

METHOD

Heat the coconut oil in a small wok or heavy-based frying pan over medium heat. Add the onions and shallow-fry for 10–12 minutes, or until the onions are dark brown and crisp. Remove with a slotted spoon and drain on paper towel. Set aside to cool.

Using a mortar and pestle (or spice grinder), pound the Maldive fish into a fine powder. Reheat the wok over medium heat and dry-roast the ground fish for 2 minutes, or until it starts to turn a little darker in colour. Transfer to a bowl and leave to cool.

Combine the roasted ground Maldive fish with the fried onions, then add the dried chilli pieces, lemon juice and a pinch of salt; mix well. Set the garnish aside until the biryani is ready to be served.

FRIED WHOLE CHICKEN WITH SPICY SAUCE

Serves 8

This dish is impressive: a whole chicken is boiled, marinated in spices and deep-fried, then served with a spicy tomato sauce. The double cooking results in a really tender, flavoursome chicken. It's a bit nerve-racking deep-frying a whole chicken, but it's not as hard as it sounds, as long as you use a decent-sized wok and don't fill it more than one-third with oil. Fareena served the chicken whole and we tore off pieces, adding it to the biryani *as we ate. It was delicious, but to be honest the* biryani *already has a lot going on and the flavours got a little lost. Try serving the chicken on its own with samba rice.*

INGREDIENTS

1.6 kg (3 lb 8 oz) whole chicken

3 teaspoons ground turmeric

salt

2 teaspoons egg yellow powdered food colouring* and/or a good pinch of saffron threads

2 tablespoons lemon juice (1 tablespoon if only using saffron)

10 cm (4 inch) piece lemongrass, white part only, very finely chopped

2 cloves garlic, thinly sliced

2 cm (¾ inch) piece ginger, thinly sliced

60 ml (2 fl oz/¼ cup) vegetable oil, plus 1 tablespoon extra

1 red onion*, sliced

1 long green chilli*, sliced lengthways three-quarters of the way, keeping it whole

1 sprig curry leaves, leaves picked

8 green cardamom pods, bruised

1 cinnamon stick, broken in half

1 teaspoon fenugreek seeds

500 g (1 lb 2 oz) roma tomatoes, finely chopped

1 small chicken stock cube, dissolved in 60 ml (2 fl oz/¼ cup) boiling water

165 g (5¾ oz/1 cup) cooked, drained and rinsed chickpeas (or tinned chickpeas), puréed with a little water

2 teaspoons garam masala

½ teaspoon ground coriander

½ teaspoon ground cumin

2 teaspoons roasted curry powder (store-bought)

125 g (4½ oz/½ cup) curd* (or thick, natural yoghurt)

2 teaspoons finely chopped mint

2 teaspoons finely chopped coriander leaves

500 ml (17 fl oz/2 cups) coconut oil*, for deep-frying

METHOD

Place the whole chicken in a stockpot, breast-side up, and cover with water. Add the turmeric and 1 teaspoon salt and bring to the boil. Reduce the heat to low, cover and gently simmer for 50 minutes, or until the chicken is cooked. Cool slightly, then carefully remove the chicken from the pot and set aside to cool to room temperature.

Combine 1 teaspoon salt, the food colouring and saffron (if using) with the lemon juice in a small bowl, then pour over the chicken. Wearing gloves, rub the marinade into the chicken, then place in the refrigerator to marinate for 2 hours.

To prepare the sauce, use a mortar and pestle to pound the lemongrass, garlic, ginger and 1 teaspoon salt into a paste. Set aside.

Heat 60 ml (2 fl oz/¼ cup) vegetable oil in a heavy-based saucepan over medium heat, add the onion and chilli and cook for 2 minutes, or until the onions are just starting to turn golden. Stir in the curry leaves and cook for a further 2 minutes. Add the cardamom pods, cinnamon stick and fenugreek seeds and cook for 1 minute. Add the extra tablespoon of oil. When the oil is hot, add the lemongrass, garlic and ginger paste and cook for 2 minutes, stirring regularly. Stir in the tomatoes and cook for 2 minutes over medium heat, then stir in the chicken stock and chickpea purée; simmer for a further 10 minutes, stirring occasionally.

In a small bowl, put the garam masala, ground coriander, cumin, curry powder and a little water (about 1 tablespoon) and mix into a thick paste. Add to the sauce and simmer over low heat for 3 minutes. Stir in the curd, 125 ml (4 fl oz/½ cup) water and the mint and coriander leaves; bring to the boil. Cover, then reduce the heat and simmer for 15–20 minutes, or until the sauce has reduced and thickened, stirring occasionally so the sauce doesn't stick to the bottom of the pan. Check for seasoning and add salt to taste (and if you find that it's too spicy, add a little extra curd).

When ready to serve, heat the coconut oil in a large wok to approximately 160°C (315°F) (a cube of bread dropped into the oil will brown in 30 seconds). Add the chicken, carefully lowering it into the oil, with the cavity facing away from you. Using a large spoon, baste the chicken with the oil every couple of minutes. It is important that the chicken heats right through as well as fries on the outside. After 7–8 minutes, carefully turn the chicken over to brown the other side. Take care with this, as the oil can splash when you turn the chicken. Cook for a further 8–10 minutes. When the chicken is golden brown with slightly charred edges, carefully remove from the wok and set aside.

Place a couple of spoonfuls of the sauce on a shallow oval-shaped dish, then carefully place the fried whole chicken on top, spooning over the remaining sauce. Serve with chicken biryani (page 34) or fragrant samba rice (page 49).

GREEN GRAM CURRY

Serves 8 as a side curry

This mild vegetarian dish, made from green gram, fresh peas, cashews and carrot, is often served with biryani. It is also delicious on its own with steamed rice.

INGREDIENTS

800 g (1 lb 12 oz) unshelled peas or 300 g (10½ oz/2 cups) shelled or frozen peas

220 g (7¾ oz/1 cup) green gram* (dried mung beans), soaked in water overnight

1 clove garlic, thinly sliced

3 cm (1¼ inch) piece ginger, thinly sliced

8 cm (3¼ inch) piece lemongrass, white part only, very finely chopped

80 ml (2½ fl oz/⅓ cup) coconut milk*, plus 250 ml (9 fl oz/1 cup) extra

1 red onion*, sliced

8 cm (3¼ inch) piece rampe (pandanus) leaf*, cut into 1 cm (½ inch) pieces

1 sprig curry leaves, leaves picked

1 thin green chilli*, sliced

pinch of freshly ground black pepper

1 tablespoon korma spice mix (store-bought)

1 teaspoon ground turmeric

1 teaspoon ground cumin

½ teaspoon salt

2 carrots, diced into small cubes

115 g (4 oz/¾ cup) raw cashew nuts

60 ml (2 fl oz/¼ cup) coconut cream*

METHOD

If using fresh peas, remove the peas from their pods and set aside. Drain the soaked green gram, then rinse and drain again. Put the green gram in a saucepan with 1.5 litres (52 fl oz/ 6 cups) water and boil for 10 minutes, or until tender. Strain and put aside.

Using a mortar and pestle, pound the garlic, ginger and lemongrass into a paste, adding a little water. Pour 80 ml (2½ fl oz/⅓ cup) coconut milk into a clay pot or heavy-based saucepan and place over medium heat, then add the onion, rampe, curry leaves, chilli, pepper and the garlic, ginger and lemongrass paste. Fry for 3–5 minutes, stirring regularly. If the spices start to stick to the bottom of the pot, add a little water.

Stir in 60 ml (2 fl oz/¼ cup) water and deglaze the pot using a wooden spoon to scrape off any browned bits stuck to the pot. Add the korma spice mix, turmeric, cumin, salt, carrots, peas, cashews, coconut cream and the extra coconut milk. Use a flat spoon to flatten and pack down the curry. Bring almost to the boil and then stir through the green gram. Reduce the heat to low, cover and cook for a further 10–15 minutes, stirring occasionally, until the green gram and carrots are cooked and the liquid has almost evaporated. Serve as a side curry with chicken biryani (page 34) or with rice.

FRAGRANT SAMBA RICE

Serves 6

Samba rice is a tiny short-grain rice grown in Sri Lanka; it has a distinct taste and slightly pungent aroma. Although it's said to be an acquired taste, preferred mainly by locals, I really enjoyed it. It is quite a starchy rice, so you need to wash it a little longer than other types, but don't worry if the water doesn't go completely clear. Infusing the rice with spices and a little ghee dissipates its pungent aroma and adds a subtle flavour that complements the rich flavours of any curry.

INGREDIENTS

480 g (1 lb 1 oz/2 cups) white samba rice*

½ teaspoon salt

1 tablespoon ghee

1 litre (35 fl oz/4 cups) water

8 cm (3¼ inch) piece rampe (pandanus) leaf*, cut in half

½ cinnamon stick

2 green cardamom pods, bruised

METHOD

Put the samba rice in a sieve and wash well under running water until the water is fairly clear. Place the rice and the remaining ingredients in a saucepan and bring to the boil. Boil for 1 minute, then cover, reduce the heat to low and simmer for 30 minutes, or until the rice is soft and all the water has been absorbed.

VATTALAPPAM

Serves 4–6

Traditionally a Tamil Muslim dish, vattalappam (or watalappan in Sinhala) is an iconic Sri Lankan dessert, similar to a steamed custard pudding, but made from jaggery, coconut milk and cardamom. When Fareena took the vattalappam out of the steamer and sprinkled over the cashews and raisins that had been fried in ghee, I had to control myself from not picking up a spoon and sneaking a taste. When I made this at home, I didn't exercise such restraint!

INGREDIENTS

210 g (7½ oz/1¼ cups) jaggery powder*

5 eggs

1 teaspoon ground cinnamon

1 teaspoon ground cardamom

good pinch of freshly grated nutmeg

¼ teaspoon salt

400 ml (14 fl oz) coconut cream*

1 teaspoon natural vanilla extract

40 g (1½ oz/¼ cup) raw cashew nuts, chopped and fried in 1 tablespoon ghee until golden

1½ tablespoons raisins

METHOD

Place the jaggery in a small heavy-based saucepan with 60 ml (2 fl oz/¼ cup) water and cook over low heat, stirring until the jaggery has dissolved. Set aside to cool a little.

In a large bowl, beat the eggs using an electric beater on low speed, then gradually beat in the cinnamon, cardamom, nutmeg and salt, followed by the coconut cream and vanilla; continue to beat for 2 minutes. Pour into a greased 1.25 litre (44 fl oz/5 cup) heatproof bowl, cover with foil and secure with a large rubber band or kitchen string.

Fill a large wok one-third full with water and place a bamboo steamer in the wok, making sure the base of the steamer isn't touching the water. Bring the water to the boil, then place the bowl in the steamer and cover with the lid. Reduce to a simmer and steam the pudding for about 1 hour, or until set. Using a thick tea towel, carefully remove the bowl from the steamer. To test if the pudding is cooked, insert a knife into the centre — it should come out clean with no pudding sticking to it.

While hot, sprinkle with fried cashews and raisins. Although traditionally served cool (the pudding deflates a little as it cools), it is delicious served warm.

FALUDA

Serves 6

Faluda is a sweet drink made from rose sherbet syrup, milk, basil seeds, vermicelli noodles and red jelly. When Fareena offered me a glass, I was a bit apprehensive because of its pink colour and musky smell, but it was delicious and really refreshing. I guzzled it down quickly, completely forgetting that it was made with Colombo tap water.

INGREDIENTS

85 g (3 oz) packet strawberry or
    raspberry jelly crystals

1 tablespoon basil seeds*

35 g (1¼ oz) dried seviyan vermicelli
    noodles*

1 litre (35 fl oz/4 cups) full-cream milk

2 tablespoons sugar

185 ml (6 fl oz/¾ cup) rose syrup (or rose
    sherbet syrup)

270 g (9½ oz/2 cups) ice cubes

METHOD

Prepare the jelly according to the instructions on the packet and set aside to cool to room temperature. Line a rectangular container (measuring approximately 12 x 20 cm/4½ x 8 inches) with plastic wrap, leaving some plastic wrap hanging over the sides. Pour the jelly into the lined container, then place in the refrigerator to set.

Soak the basil seeds in 500 ml (17 fl oz/2 cups) cold water for 15 minutes, or until soft and plump. While the seeds are soaking, bring 500 ml (17 fl oz/2 cups) water to the boil in a saucepan, add the vermicelli noodles and cook for 2–3 minutes, or until tender. Drain, rinse under cold running water to stop the cooking process, then drain and set aside.

Bring the milk to the boil in a large heavy-based saucepan. Stir in the sugar, then reduce the heat and simmer over low heat for 2–3 minutes, or until the sugar has dissolved. Remove from the heat and stir in the rose syrup, and set aside to cool slightly.

Drain the basil seeds and add to the faluda, followed by the vermicelli noodles. Transfer to a large jug or container and chill in the refrigerator.

When the faluda is chilled, carefully remove the jelly from the container and cut into 2 cm (¾ inch) cubes. Take six tall glasses and fill each one halfway with the jelly and ice cubes, then pour over the faluda. Serve as a drink or dessert.

THE FESTIVAL OF LIGHTS
Vesak

The city is alive with excitement and a sense of anticipation that something big is about to happen, and it's impossible not to get carried along with it. Today is the start of Vesak, the festival of lights, held annually on the full moon in May, celebrating the birth, enlightenment and death of Buddha.

Over the past week, Colombo has been busily preparing for tonight and now the entire city is adorned with decorations. Shops, buildings, hotels and temples are draped in fairy lights. Colourful lanterns and Buddhist flags hang along the streets and in front of homes, and the aroma of burning oil lamps and incense wafts across the city. *Pandals* as large as billboards have been erected, decorated with thousands of multicoloured light globes surrounding images that depict stories of Buddha's life.

Although the festival does not officially begin until the *pandal* lights are turned on, some activities have already started, adding to the excitement. Temples are overflowing with white-clad devotees taking worship, listening to teachings and giving offerings.

Sounds of firecrackers can be heard in sporadic bursts across the city. Sajeeva, my Buddhist tuk-tuk driver, tells me that they are to let people know when a *dansal*, a free food stall, is ready to start giving away food and drink. No sooner does he finish his explanation than there is another loud burst of firecrackers. We drive quickly down the street, following the direction of the noise.

The first *dansal* we come across is at a nearby school, giving away free ice cream. About one hundred people are queued up, all jostling to get to the front, with outstretched arms reaching over one another, their noise and chatter almost drowned out by the religious music blaring through loudspeakers.

Two ice creams later, we are back in the tuk-tuk, hurrying down the streets. As we approach a busy intersection in Nugegoda, we spot a long queue that snakes down the road. This is a *dansal* given by the owners of the local hardware store, and a section of footpath outside the shop has been cordoned off. They haven't started handing out food just yet, but I can see boxes piled high with *roti* and large jugs of tea. When the owner finishes giving a speech from a crackling microphone, the monk beside him uses a candle to light an oil lamp, then passes the candle to the owner, who does the same. This signals that the *dansal* is now open. Loud, pulsing music begins to play, and people push and shove to get to the front of the line, only relaxing once they have a cup of tea and a *roti* in their hands.

We jump back in the tuk-tuk and drive through the suburbs, along the way sampling some of the best vegetarian food I have ever eaten. At a Buddhist temple in Nawala, we eat boiled manioc and *lunu miris*, a spicy onion and chilli *sambol*. At a music store in Boralesgamuwa, I have my first glass of *kola kenda*, a delicious porridge-like drink made from leafy greens, red rice and coconut milk.

In Kirulapone, Sajeeva briefly stops to visit his mum, and she insists we have a glass of *inguru koththamalli* (coriander and ginger tea) from the *dansal* near her house. This stall appears even more popular than the others we have visited and it's literally stopping traffic. Men, carrying trays laden with small plastic cups of tea, carefully make their way along the side of the road, passing tea to people on motorbikes and through car windows.

When we reach the city centre, around Beira Lake, the streets have filled to maximum capacity. It's not just the people from Colombo who are here, but others from nearby villages, who have arrived in lorries, tractors and buses. Some don't get out of their lorries, choosing instead to watch the activities from inside, which they have cleverly decked out with lounges, chairs, cushions and rugs.

With the conclusion of the 6 pm prayer at Gangaramaya Temple, devotees spill out onto the street next to the lake. A female choir, dressed in white and holding Buddhist flags, sings on an outdoor stage opposite the lake. Nearby, large hand-crafted lanterns come to life, all trying to outshine each other and win this year's Vesak lantern competition.

> *'We jump back in the tuk-tuk and drive through the suburbs, along the way sampling some of the best vegetarian food I have ever eaten.'*

When the main *pandal* next to the temple is finally turned on, the crowd erupts with clapping and cheering — the festival has officially begun. A burst of fireworks lights up the sky, and the crowd moves as a pack towards the lake's edge, everyone hoping to secure a good vantage point.

Boats covered in fairy lights set off across the lake, drifting peacefully between the floating illuminated lotus flowers. A bridge, adorned with tiny blue lights, opens and people stream in single file across it to a floating garden.

The garden and lake look incredibly beautiful lit up against the night sky, adding a fairytale feel to the festivities. Now the excitement has reached a crescendo, a sense of calm falls over the crowd. Colombo during Vesak is truly mesmerising and leaves an impression on me that will last forever.

MANIOC WITH LUNU MIRIS

Serves 4

Lunu miris is a fiery hot onion and chilli sambol served as a condiment with many Sri Lankan dishes. During Vesak, it was served with boiled manioc for dansal at the Wickramasingharamaya Temple in Nawala. Dansal is a public almsgiving where free food and drinks are offered. Local devotees boiled the manioc in massive vats over an open fire in the temple gardens. They didn't add any Maldive fish to the lunu miris, as the monks are strict vegetarians, but traditionally it's usually included. I was surprised that none of the monks helped with the cooking, but I soon learnt that monks don't prepare their own meals; all their meals are cooked and donated by local families.

LUNU MIRIS
1 tablespoon Maldive fish pieces*
  (preferably flakes) (optional)
1 tablespoon dried chilli pieces*
salt
½ red onion*, very finely chopped
juice of ½ lime

MANIOC
650 g (1 lb 7 oz) manioc* (cassava)
  (or 600 g/1 lb 5 oz frozen)
1 teaspoon ground turmeric
kanda leaf*, to serve (or banana leaf)

METHOD
To make the lunu miris, use a mortar and pestle (or spice grinder) to pound the Maldive fish into a coarse powder. Add the dried chilli pieces, ½ teaspoon salt and onion, then continue pounding until all the ingredients are mixed together to form a fine paste. Stir in the lime juice and mix well. (This will keep for a few days in the refrigerator.) Set aside.

Peel the fresh manioc and cut into 3 cm (1¼ inch) cubes. To prevent discolouring, fill a large bowl with water, stir in the turmeric, then add the chopped manioc and mix. Set aside. If using frozen manioc, this has already been peeled and it doesn't need to be placed in the turmeric water. Frozen manioc is hard to cut, so let it defrost a little first, or alternatively, cut after it has been boiled.

Bring a large saucepan of water to the boil, add 1½ teaspoons salt and the drained manioc. Cook over medium heat for 10 minutes, or until tender. Drain and serve warm on a kanda leaf, and top with a small spoonful of lunu miris.

GINGER & CORIANDER TEA

Serves 4

I had my first cup of ginger and coriander tea at a dansal in Kirulapone that Sajeeva, my Sinhalese tuk-tuk driver, took me to. It was delicious, and judging by the number of tuk-tuks, motorbikes, cars and buses that stopped for a cup, everyone else thought so too. The tea is believed to have many medicinal benefits and is used as a remedy for colds, sore throats and muscle pain.

INGREDIENTS

50 g (1¾ oz/heaped ½ cup) coriander
   seeds, washed

40 g (1½ oz) piece ginger, roughly sliced
sugar or honey, to taste

METHOD

Combine the coriander seeds and ginger in a saucepan with 1 litre (35 fl oz/4 cups) water. Bring to the boil, reduce the heat to medium and simmer, uncovered, for 15 minutes. Strain and add sugar to taste, stir well and serve.

KOLA KENDA

Serves 6

Kola kenda is a porridge-like drink made from red rice, coconut milk and the juice of leafy greens. The first time I tried it was at a dansal in Boralesgamuwa. They served it warm in glasses with a small piece of jaggery, which you nibble on between sips. There was a number of different flavours of kola kenda being served, each made from a different blend of leafy greens, but the most popular (and traditional) was made from gotu kola.

INGREDIENTS

165 g (5¾ oz/¾ cup) red rice*

250 ml (9 fl oz/1 cup) juice from gotu
    kola* (you will need about 750 g
    (1 lb 10 oz) of gotu kola or use
    a mixture of English spinach,
    watercress and parsley)

375 ml (13 fl oz/1½ cups) coconut milk*

pinch of salt

jaggery pieces*, to serve

METHOD

Wash the rice well, then place in a saucepan with 1 litre (35 fl oz/4 cups) water and bring to the boil. Reduce the heat to low, then cover and simmer for 30 minutes, or until the rice is well cooked and mushy.

While the rice is cooking, prepare the gotu kola juice. Wash the gotu kola, trim off and discard the bottom 5 cm (2 inches) of stem, then push the rest through the juicer. You will need 250 ml (9 fl oz/1 cup) juice (see note).

Stir the coconut milk into the rice, and add about 125 ml (4 fl oz/½ cup) extra water if needed (the kola kenda needs to be thick but runny). Simmer, uncovered, for 5 minutes, or until the rice reaches a thin porridge-like consistency. Stir in the juice and a pinch of salt, bring to just below the boil, then remove from the heat. Serve hot with a piece of jaggery.

NOTE: In Sri Lanka, to extract the gotu kola juice, the leaves are puréed in batches in a blender, then strained through a fine sieve, discarding the pulp. Using a juicer gives a more intense flavour. If you don't have a juicer, ask your greengrocer or juice bar to juice the leaves for you.

CENTRAL
Up Country

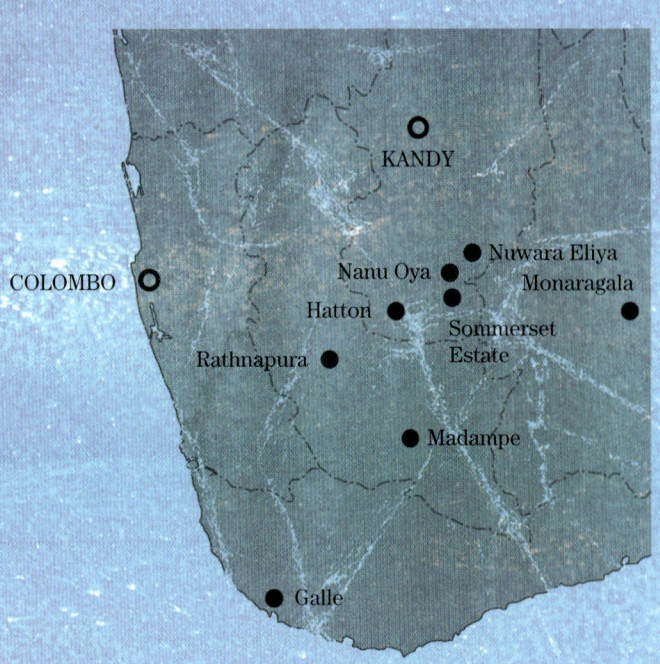

Sri Lanka's lush inland hill country, known to the locals as Up Country, is picture perfect with mist-shrouded mountains, plunging waterfalls, quaint hilltop villages, lavish Colonial plantation bungalows, and a seamless carpet of rolling green tea fields, embroidered with sari-clad tea pickers.

At lunchtime, groups of tea pickers can be found enjoying parcels of rice and curry and sipping strong black tea from old arrack bottles. Most tea pickers are Tamil, belonging to a group known as Plantation Tamils, and speak a slightly different dialect to the Jaffna Tamils. The region is also home to the old Sinhalese kingdom of Kandy, which remains the Buddhist cultural and spiritual hub of Sri Lanka. Fortunately, the region has managed to escape much devastation from the war and it is easy to forget about the former conflict here.

The cuisine of the Up Country is simple and fresh, utilising the abundance of locally grown fruit and vegetables. Fewer fragrant spices and less coconut milk are used compared to other regions in Sri Lanka, where they are more readily available.

SINHALESE & TAMIL NEW YEAR
Aluth Avurudu & Puthandu

There is no better opportunity than a national festival to showcase the wonderful food of Sri Lanka. New Year is a chance to taste an array of delicious traditional dishes, most of which are packed with an alarming amount of sugar and deep-fried. Called 'sweetmeats', these are enjoyed as part of the first meal of the New Year and throughout the celebrations. At New Year, sweetmeats are to Sri Lankans what champagne is to Westerners.

Known as 'Aluth Avurudu' in Sinhala and 'Puthandu' in Tamil, New Year is celebrated in mid-April and does not fall at midnight, but at an auspicious time calculated by astrologers. Celebrations last for over a week, with most businesses closing for a well-earned break. A few days before New Year, there is a flurry of last-minute shopping as people flock to the streets to buy gifts and clothing. Public transport becomes packed as people leave the cities to return home to their villages.

Although the Sinhalese Buddhists and Tamil Hindus have their own distinct religious ceremonies, many of their rituals and traditions are similar, with most events taking place at a carefully calculated time. The most significant of these are the lighting of the hearth and boiling of the milk, which take place at the 'dawn of the New Year'; and the first meal of the New Year, which is enjoyed a few hours later. The precise time for the first meal is different for the Sinhalese and Tamils, and they each have their own traditional dishes. Special colours are worn and directions followed for different rituals, to ensure good fortune for the coming year. Gifts, usually clothes, are exchanged and blessings given to family and friends.

In the period before New Year, houses are cleaned, oil lamps are lit, debts are paid off and old grudges settled. The Tamil Hindus apply a herbal water as part of their pre New Year rituals, and the Sinhalese Buddhists participate in a national oil anointing ceremony, but this occurs a few days later. Both communities return to work a week after New Year at the same auspicious time, however the direction in which they must leave their homes for work is different.

With so many rituals taking place and each with its own symbolism, Sri Lankan New Year can be very confusing, but it is a lot of fun. Rather than try to make sense of everything, I found it easier to just relax and immerse myself in the unfamiliarity of all the traditions and to enjoy the colour, culture and cuisine of the celebrations.

TAMIL CELEBRATIONS
Mahalukshmi

I am standing among a crowd of women wrapped in vibrant silk saris, while barefoot men in white sarongs vigorously smash coconuts on the street. Coconut pieces and coconut water are flying everywhere, smudging bindis and splattering newly purchased saris. Men with shovels scurry in to scoop up the shells, but no sooner are they cleared away than more appear.

It is just after sunrise and I am with hundreds of Hindus on Sea Street in Colombo, to mark the beginning of the festivities for Puthandu, the Tamil New Year.

When all the coconut shells have been swept away, two large, brightly decorated chariots appear, pulled by devotees, followed by a smaller chariot drawn by cows. Each chariot carries a statue of the elephant-headed god, Lord Pillaiyar (also known as Ganesh), the god of wisdom, prosperity and good fortune.

The chariots come to a halt and the crowd chants as the *kovil* (temple) priest (*kurukkal*) drapes flower garlands and gold-threaded silk cloth over the statues. Offerings of coconuts, fruit, flowers, betel leaves, rosewater, incense and silk are handed up on a tray to the *kurukkal*, who blesses them and hands them back to the crowd. These offerings are to thank Lord Pillaiyar for the good fortune bestowed on them during the year and to receive a blessing for a prosperous year ahead.

Accompanied by the sounds of musicians, drumming and chanting, the chariots move a few metres and then stop again as more offerings are made. Meanwhile, more coconuts are smashed on the road ahead and then swept away, allowing the chariots to continue their procession. The breaking of coconuts symbolises the release of bad energy or karma that may be holding you back, allowing you to move forward in life. The white flesh of the coconut symbolises a pure heart.

After a few hours I leave the chariot procession behind and make my way to the Up Country, as I have been invited to spend the New Year holiday there. It's a slow five-hour journey along winding and bumpy mountain roads, but the scenery is breathtakingly beautiful. Lush green tea fields cover mountains that disappear into the mist and at every couple of bends there are roadside stalls selling home-grown vegetables and unusual looking fruits. It's quite late in the afternoon when we arrive in Hatton.

In a small house next door to the town's main *kovil*, I am greeted by a plump, jolly woman called Mahalukshmi. She gives me such a cheerful welcome that I feel as if I've known her for years, yet this is the first time we've met. Her husband is

75

one of the *kurukkal* and he is at the *kovil* preparing for tonight's ceremony, while Mahalukshmi is busy cooking at home for the *kovil* feast.

The preparations for the feast are well under way, but before I can join in, Mahalukshmi lays out an array of dishes and insists I sit down and eat. There are deep-fried lentil patties (*vadai*), boiled chickpeas fried with mild spices and fresh coconut (*soundal*), and a rice pudding sweetened with jaggery (*pongal*). Mahalukshmi disappears into the kitchen, returning with a small cup of warm sago (*payasam*). It is divine — sweet and creamy, with a distinct cardamom flavour. As I sip my sago, savouring the flavours, Mahalukshmi explains how any cooking for the *kovil* must take place in their home to ensure it is 'pure and clean', and that all the ingredients must be good quality.

After eating I join Mahalukshmi, her sister-in-law Annapoorani, and their good friend Valliyamma. The women sit cross-legged on the bedroom floor, spooning filling into flattened balls of dough and shaping them into little parcels, their hands working rhythmically and with ease.

'We are making *mothagam*,' Mahalukshmi explains. 'It is believed to be Lord Pillaiyar's favourite dish, and they are offered to him in worship.' Pointing to a colourful picture of the elephant-headed god on the wall, she says, 'He is holding a plate of *mothagam* in his hand. The outer dough is said to represent the world, and the filling is the life of the people, like us.'

'The women sit cross-legged on the bedroom floor, spooning filling into flattened balls of dough and shaping them into little parcels, their hands working rhythmically and with ease.'

Mothagam are sweet dumplings, stuffed with fresh coconut, green gram, jaggery and spices. They are a traditional Tamil New Year sweetmeat, but are sometimes served at other special occasions and celebrations.

Seeing that I am intrigued by the way the dumplings are shaped, Valliyamma explains, 'The shape should be like the belly of the elephant and the top like the trunk.' I have a go, but it's not quite as easy as it looks. Thankfully Valliyamma is patient and soon my dumplings are good enough to join the production line.

Soon it's time to steam the dumplings, but I'm disappointed to learn that I will have to wait until after the *kovil* ceremony before I can taste one, as it is a tradition that the *mothagam* are first offered to Lord Pillaiyar before they are shared among the devotees.

PAYASAM

Serves 8

Payasam (sago) is an essential sweet dish at any Tamil celebration or festival, including New Year and weddings. It is usually served in small stainless-steel cups, but the traditional way to serve it is on a banana leaf and topped with crushed pappadum. The best payasam I tasted was Mahalukshmi's; it was wonderfully thick and creamy, infused with cardamom and topped with cashews and raisins.

INGREDIENTS

¾ tablespoon green gram*
  (dried mung beans)

1 tablespoon ghee, plus 1 tablespoon extra

200 g (7 oz/1 cup) sago (payasam)

30 g (1 oz) dried seviyan vermicelli
  noodles*

2 tablespoons roughly chopped raw
  cashew nuts

1 tablespoon raisins

pinch of salt

875 ml (30 fl oz/3½ cups) coconut milk*

200 g (7 oz) caster sugar

1 teaspoon ground cardamom

125 ml (4 fl oz/½ cup) coconut cream*

METHOD

Dry-roast the green gram in a heavy-based frying pan over medium heat for 4 minutes. Remove and set aside to cool slightly. Using a mortar and pestle (or spice grinder), pound the green gram into a fine powder. Set aside.

Melt the ghee in the frying pan and fry the sago over medium heat for 3 minutes, or until it starts to puff and pop. Add the vermicelli noodles and fry for 1 minute, or until golden brown, stirring continuously so the vermicelli doesn't burn. Remove and set aside. Fry the cashews and raisins in the extra ghee over low heat for 1–2 minutes until golden, then remove with a slotted spoon and drain on paper towel.

Bring 875 ml (30 fl oz/3½ cups) water to the boil in a large saucepan. Add a pinch of salt, then quickly add the sago and vermicelli and stir well. Simmer for 18 minutes over low–medium heat, stirring regularly, until it thickens and the sago is cooked and turns transparent (stir continuously for the last 5 minutes so the sago doesn't catch on the bottom of the pan). Add a little more water if needed.

Add the coconut milk, bring almost to the boil, then reduce the heat to low and simmer for 3 minutes, stirring continuously, until the mixture starts to thicken slightly. Stir in the green gram powder and simmer for 3–4 minutes. Add the sugar, cardamom and coconut cream and cook for 4–5 minutes, stirring, until the mixture thickens a little. Stir in the fried cashews and raisins or sprinkle them on top. Serve hot in small cups.

PONGAL
Serves 8

This sweet rice pudding is a traditional Tamil New Year dessert and is also served at other auspicious ceremonies and special occasions. One morning, when I was walking along the beach in Point Pedro, I came across an entire village eating pongal from banana leaves. A local fisherman had recently purchased a new boat, and his wife had set up her cooking equipment on the beach, lit a fire and made a large pot of pongal. Making pongal for everyone was a way to share their joy with the community and to bless their boat with prosperity.

INGREDIENTS

55 g (2 oz/¼ cup) green gram*
  (dried mung beans)

2 tablespoons ghee, plus 1 tablespoon extra

80 g (2¾ oz/½ cup) raw cashew nuts,
  roughly chopped, plus 40 g (1½ oz/
  ¼ cup) extra (left whole), to garnish

50 g (1¾ oz/⅓ cup) raisins

420 g (15 oz/2 cups) red rice*

½ teaspoon salt

260 g (9¼ oz/1½ cups) jaggery powder*

8 cardamom pods, pounded into a powder
  (or ¼ teaspoon ground cardamom)

120 g (4¼ oz/1 cup) freshly
  scraped coconut*

250 ml (9 fl oz/1 cup) coconut milk*

125 ml (4 fl oz/½ cup) coconut cream*

METHOD

Dry-roast the green gram in a heavy-based frying pan over medium heat for 4 minutes. Remove and set aside to cool slightly. Using a mortar and pestle, pound the green gram until they split, then set aside.

Melt the ghee in the frying pan over medium heat, add the chopped cashews and raisins and fry for 1–2 minutes, stirring until golden. Remove with a slotted spoon. Add the whole cashews and fry until golden. Remove and set aside to cool (these will be used for garnishing).

Wash the red rice thoroughly in cold water. Bring 1.5 litres (52 fl oz/6 cups) water to the boil in a large heavy-based saucepan. Add the red rice, green gram and salt. Stir to combine, bring back to the boil, then reduce the heat to low, cover and simmer for 15–20 minutes, or until the rice is tender (the consistency should be quite slushy; add more boiling water if needed).

Add the jaggery powder and simmer, uncovered, over low heat until the jaggery dissolves and the mixture starts to bubble. Stir continuously, so the mixture doesn't catch on the bottom of the pan. Add the cardamom, fried cashews and raisins, coconut and the extra ghee, and mix to combine. Simmer for 2 minutes, stirring continuously. Slowly add the coconut milk and cream, continuing to stir. Simmer for 1 minute, or until the consistency is thick and sticky. Serve warm and garnish with the extra cashew nuts.

MOTHAGAM

Makes 30 balls

Mothagam *are delicious, sweet dumplings filled with a mixture of green gram, spices, coconut and jaggery. When I went to a Sri Lankan shop in Sydney and told the Tamil owner I was making* mothagam, *he chuckled in disbelief. But when I returned and told him they were a success, he announced to all his customers that I could make* mothagam *and gave me a generous discount.*

FILLING

110 g (3¾ oz/½ cup) green gram* (dried
   mung beans), soaked in water overnight

120 g (4¼ oz/1 cup) freshly scraped
   coconut*

1 teaspoon fennel seeds

85 g (3 oz/½ cup) jaggery powder*

2 teaspoons ground cinnamon

1 teaspoon ground cardamom

60 g (2¼ oz) white sugar cubes

DOUGH

250 g (9 oz/1⅔ cups) plain flour

480 g (1 lb 1 oz/4 cups) fine red
   rice flour*

pinch of salt

about 750 ml (26 fl oz/3 cups) boiling
   water

1½ tablespoons coconut oil*, plus extra
   for cooking

METHOD

To make the filling, drain the soaked green gram, then rinse and drain again. Put the gram in a saucepan with 500 ml (17 fl oz/2 cups) water and bring to the boil. Cover, then reduce the heat and simmer for 10–15 minutes, or until tender and starting to break up. Drain and set aside.

In a heavy-based frying pan over medium heat, dry-roast the coconut for 7–10 minutes, stirring continuously, until dark golden brown. Remove from the pan. Dry-roast the fennel seeds for 1 minute, then pound into a powder using a mortar and pestle (or spice grinder).

In a heavy-based saucepan over medium heat, melt the jaggery, adding a small amount of water (about 1½ tablespoons); continue to stir. When the jaggery has melted, stir in the roasted coconut and boiled green gram, then add the ground fennel, cinnamon and cardamom. Reduce the heat to low and very slowly add the sugar cubes, a couple at a time, stirring them through the mixture with a wooden spoon as they soften. Remove from the heat and set aside.

To prepare the dough, place the plain flour in a bamboo steamer lined with two layers of muslin or a piece of non-stick baking paper. Fill a wok about one-third full with water and bring to the boil. Place the steamer in the wok, ensuring the bottom of the steamer isn't touching the water, and heat the flour (uncovered) for 4 minutes, or until the flour is warm, stirring occasionally with a fork to break up any lumps. Sift the warm flour into a large mixing bowl. Sift the red rice flour into the same bowl, add a pinch of salt, then mix together.

Using a wooden spoon, gradually stir in the boiling water, using just enough to make a thick, pliable dough. Mix in the coconut oil, then gradually add 80 ml (2½ fl oz/⅓ cup) cold water; knead with your hands to make a pliable dough. Allow the dough to cool slightly. Take a small handful of dough (about 50 g/1¾ oz) and roll it into a ball the size of a small lime. Repeat with the remaining dough and then loosely cover the balls with plastic wrap so they don't dry out.

Grease your hands with a little coconut oil. Take a ball of dough and flatten it in the palm of your hand into a disc about 4 mm (⅛ inch) thick. Then, starting in the centre of the disc, use your thumb to press the dough outwards into a cup shape. Place a heaped teaspoon of filling into the centre of the dough cup and press it down with your index finger, then press the edges of the dough cup to thin them. Bring the edges together at the top and pinch to seal, then pull gently to form a small point on top. Repeat with the rest of the mixture, making sure to re-grease your hands with coconut oil for each ball.

Steam in batches in a bamboo steamer lined with two layers of muslin, making sure to place them 5–10 mm (¼–½ inch) apart so they don't stick together. Steam for 10–15 minutes, or until cooked (the outer layer should go shiny when they're ready). Carefully transfer to a serving dish and serve warm or cold.

SINHALESE CELEBRATIONS
Priyantha & Thiloma

I am fortunate to be invited to share the first meal of the New Year with a Sinhalese Buddhist family in Hatton. Priyantha and his wife, Thiloma, live in a large modern house, with their two young sons, on the edge of the valley.

I arrive at their home around 10 pm, shortly before the auspicious time decreed for the New Year meal. The family warmly welcomes me and Priyantha proudly shows me around their newly built two-storey home. The television is blaring with the national New Year countdown, as the family patiently waits for the precise time when they can begin the meal.

I notice there are over a dozen clocks in the dining room and jokingly ask Priyantha if he is worried he might miss the auspicious time. 'No, no. I have a clock repair business in Hatton,' he explains with a chuckle. Priyantha also works as an agent for the Development Lotteries Board and is a member of the local government for the Hatton and Dickoya areas.

As the countdown draws closer, everyone helps to put the food on the table, which is covered in a white linen tablecloth and decorated with flowers, a large bowl of bananas and a small oil lamp. It is an impressive feast of over ten different dishes. All of them except one are sweetmeats. There is *kiri bath* (milk rice), *seeni sambol* (sweet onion *sambol*), *kokis* (crisp fried biscuits), *konda kavum* (deep-fried oil cakes), *aluwa* (roasted rice flour and sugar slice), *mung keyum* (green gram and treacle cakes), *pani walalu* (deep-fried coils of batter drenched in sugar syrup), *dodol* (rich jaggery and coconut jelly), milk toffee and butter cake.

I can sense there is something worrying Thiloma. When I ask, I learn that earlier in the evening when the family performed the boiling of the milk ritual, the milk did not boil over properly and, as a result, she is worried that the year ahead may not be prosperous. 'The milk should have boiled over and spilled down the side of the pot as a symbol of abundance and prosperity for the household,' Thiloma explains.

When the final ten-second countdown is about to begin, the family excitedly gathers around the table. At exactly 10.28 pm, the TV loudly announces, '*Suba Aluth Avurudhak Veva!*' 'Happy New Year' everyone enthusiastically shouts in unison. Priyantha lights the first wick on the oil lamp and Thiloma lights the second. Each of the boys also lights a wick, and I am touched when they ask me to do the same.

Priyantha hands his wife a betel leaf with some money on top and she returns the gesture. They then each perform the ritual with their sons. This ritual is called

ganu-dhenu, meaning 'give and take'. The boys bow down and touch their parents' feet as a mark of respect, and in turn, the parents bless them. Priyantha then heads into his office to carry out his first business transaction for the New Year, and the boys open their school books. This only lasts a few minutes and is more a ceremonial gesture than anything else.

Finally it is time to sit down and eat. Priyantha takes a slice of *kiri bath*, which he hand-feeds to his wife, and then to each of his children. Thiloma does the same for her husband and their children. Priyantha piles up a plate of *kiri bath* for me, but thankfully he doesn't try to hand-feed me. I tuck in; it is creamy and comforting, and the rice has a delicious richness from being cooked in coconut milk. I relish the flavours when combined with the *seeni sambol*, a caramelised onion *sambol*, which has a slight chilli kick and a saltiness from the dried Maldive fish.

More food is piled on my plate; this time it's *konda kavum*, which Priyantha insists I must try with a small banana. The *konda kavum* has a distinct sweetness from being fried in coconut oil, and is lightly spiced with fennel and cardamom. Eating them with the banana brings the flavour of the spices to the fore.

> *'I relish the flavours when combined with the* seeni sambol, *a caramelised onion* sambol, *which has a slight chilli kick and a saltiness from the dried Maldive fish.'*

Although I am quite full, the *dodol* is intriguing me. It looks like dark brown jelly and I have seen it for sale but have always been put off by its appearance. I take a small slice — it is surprisingly delicious and tastes more like a pudding than jelly.

Because I have helped myself to the *dodol*, Priyantha obviously thinks I am still hungry, as he starts piling more food on my plate. When he reaches for the *pani walalu*, I signal for him to stop. I have eaten these fried coils of batter before; drenched in a sticky sugar syrup, they are sickly sweet and even I know my limits! But I weaken and try a small piece — I have to at least taste a little of everything on the New Year table.

I have eaten more sugar than my body can handle, but still I can't help but think about the food and what ingredients are in each dish. Of all the food I have eaten tonight, the standout was the *seeni sambol*. When Thiloma asks if I'd like to come back the next day to learn how to cook it, I quickly accept her offer.

KIRI BATH

Makes 15 pieces

Kiri bath *(milk rice)* is a traditional Sinhalese dish served at almost all festivals, ceremonies and special occasions. Watching Priyantha feed his wife a piece of kiri bath *with his own hand was bizarre and rather uncomfortable. I would run a million miles if someone tried to hand-feed me, but this is an age-old tradition in Sri Lanka and it is believed to bring good luck and strengthen family unity.

INGREDIENTS

440 g (15½ oz/2 cups) medium-grain
   white rice

pinch of salt

500 ml (17 fl oz/2 cups) coconut milk*

250 ml (9 fl oz/1 cup) coconut cream*

METHOD

Wash the rice well and place in a saucepan with enough water to cover the rice by 2.5 cm (1 inch). Add a pinch of salt and bring to the boil. Stir through the coconut milk and bring back to the boil, then reduce the heat to low, cover and simmer for 15–20 minutes, or until the rice is cooked (the rice should be moist and sticky). Stir in the coconut cream and cook for a further 3–5 minutes, uncovered, stirring occasionally, until the coconut cream has been absorbed.

Pour into a lightly greased 20 x 30 cm (8 x 12 inch) tray or large shallow dish. Flatten down the rice with a spatula, and allow to cool slightly for 15 minutes. Kiri bath is traditionally cut into diamonds or squares, and served warm or cold topped with a spoonful of seeni sambol (page 94) or lunu miris (page 61).

SEENI SAMBOL

Makes 220 g (7¾ oz/1 cup)

I adore this mild onion sambol. The sweetness from the caramelised onions and sugar (seeni) is perfectly balanced with chilli and spices. One of the key ingredients is dried Maldive fish, which adds a saltiness and distinct Sri Lankan flavour. Thiloma gave me a jar of seeni sambol to take on my drive around the island. I would stop at roadside stalls, order some pol roti or egg hoppers and inconspicuously produce the jar from my bag and smear on the sambol — it was heavenly!

INGREDIENTS

¾ tablespoon Maldive fish pieces*
  (preferably flakes)

1½ tablespoons coconut oil*

10 cm (4 inch) piece rampe (pandanus)
  leaf*, cut into 2 cm (¾ inch) pieces

2 sprigs curry leaves, leaves picked

1 cinnamon stick, broken in half

2 thin green chillies*, sliced into thirds

4 red onions*, halved and thinly sliced

1 teaspoon salt

1½ teaspoons ground turmeric

1½ teaspoons dry sambol mix
  (store-bought) (or dried chilli pieces*)

1 tablespoon sugar

METHOD

Using a mortar and pestle (or spice grinder), pound the Maldive fish pieces into a coarse powder and set aside.

Heat the coconut oil in a small wok or heavy-based saucepan over medium heat. Add the rampe, curry leaves, cinnamon stick, chillies, onions and salt; cook for 6–8 minutes, stirring regularly, until the onions are golden and almost caramelised.

Stir in the turmeric, sambol mix and ground Maldive fish, then stir in the sugar and cook for a further 3–5 minutes, stirring regularly so the spices don't stick to the wok (add a little water if needed). Remove the cinnamon sticks and discard them. Cool to room temperature before serving.

KONDA KAVUM

Makes about 30

Konda kavum *are little deep-fried oil cakes made from rice flour, treacle and spices. Creating a well-shaped* konda kavum *requires considerable practice and even Thiloma had to call in the local* konda kavum *expert to show me the technique. The cakes should have a knot on the top, which emulates the hair bun (*konda*) of the native women. I only managed to produce a few that were the right shape, but they all tasted delicious even if they were a bit misshapen.*

INGREDIENTS

1½ teaspoons fennel seeds

1½ teaspoons aniseeds

2½ teaspoons ground cardamom

480 g (1 lb 1 oz/4 cups) fine red rice flour*

110 g (3¾ oz/¾ cup) plain flour

115 g (4 oz/½ cup) caster sugar

1 teaspoon salt

750 ml (26 fl oz/3 cups) treacle*

375 ml (13 fl oz/1½ cups) coconut oil*,
  for deep-frying

METHOD

Dry-roast the fennel seeds and aniseeds in a heavy-based frying pan over low heat for 3 minutes. Remove from the heat and allow to cool slightly. Using a mortar and pestle (or spice grinder), pound the seeds into a fine powder. Stir in the ground cardamom.

Sift the red rice flour and plain flour into a large mixing bowl, add the sugar, salt and ground spices and stir to combine. Gradually whisk in 250 ml (9 fl oz/1 cup) of the treacle and then whisk in 625 ml (21½ fl oz/2½ cups) warm water, about 125 ml (4 fl oz/½ cup) at a time. Add the remaining treacle, a little at a time, whisking to combine (the consistency should be smooth but thicker than pancake batter). Set aside for 1 hour.

Heat the coconut oil in a small wok or heavy-based saucepan to approximately 180°C (350°F) (a cube of bread dropped into the oil will brown in 15 seconds). Place a small fluted brioche mould (about 4 cm (1½ inch) in diameter) into the wok, ensuring it is fully submerged in the oil, then very slowly pour 80 ml (2½ fl oz/⅓ cup) of batter into the mould. While you are pouring, use your other hand to spoon over the hot oil. Continue spooning over the oil, then when the top of the cake starts to cook, insert a skewer in the middle (without piercing the whole way through) and start rotating the skewer and moving it up and down — the uncooked batter will start moving up the skewer. Continue to rotate the skewer and spoon over the oil, making sure to get the hot oil into the hole created by the skewer. Using a flat spoon, press down on the outer sides of the cake to help shape it. When golden brown (it takes about 3 minutes to fry each cake), turn the cake over to release it from the mould, then fry for a further 20 seconds. Remove with a slotted spoon and drain on paper towel. Serve warm or cold.

KOKIS

Makes about 50

These thin, crisp biscuits, made from a deep-fried batter of rice flour and coconut milk, are traditionally shaped like a wheel. Originally a Dutch recipe, they are now considered an authentic Sri Lankan sweetmeat, often served for special occasions such as New Year. They are easy to make, but you will need a special kokis *mould, which you can buy from most Sri Lankan specialty stores.*

INGREDIENTS

330 g (11½ oz/1½ cups) medium-grain white rice

270 ml (9½ fl oz) coconut cream*

1½ teaspoons ground turmeric

2 teaspoons sugar

1 teaspoon salt

1 egg, whisked lightly

500 ml (17 fl oz/2 cups) coconut oil*, for cooking

METHOD

To make rice flour, first wash the rice well and drain. Process the wet rice in a food processor on high until it turns into a coarse flour. Sift into a large bowl to get rid of any lumps, then return the flour and any unprocessed rice to the food processor and process on high, then sift again. Repeat this process another two or three times until most of the rice has turned into flour. Discard any unprocessed rice left in the sieve at the end (don't worry if this is about ½ cup, as you will still have enough).

Place the rice flour into a bowl and gradually whisk in the coconut cream. Whisk in the turmeric, sugar and salt. Add the egg and whisk until fully combined. The consistency should be smooth like pancake batter, but a little thicker; add a little extra coconut cream if needed.

Heat the coconut oil in a wok or heavy-based saucepan to approximately 180°C (350°F) (a cube of bread dropped into the oil will brown in 15 seconds). Dip the kokis mould in the hot oil for a few seconds to heat it up, then dip into the batter (see note). Be careful not to cover the very top of the mould in batter or it will be difficult to remove the kokis. Gently shake off any excess batter and submerge in the oil for 2–3 minutes, or until the batter is almost cooked, then use a metal skewer to gently release the biscuit from the mould. Cook for a further 2 minutes until light golden, then remove with a skewer or slotted spoon and drain on paper towel.

Kokis are usually served with a number of other sweetmeats, but are delicious eaten as a biscuit with a cup of spicy Ceylon tea (page 18). Store in an airtight container.

NOTE: As you use up the batter, transfer it to a smaller bowl so you are still able to dip the mould into the batter to the right depth.

LUNCH WITH THE TEA PICKERS
Mary

With the morning's harvest weighed and bagged, it is now lunchtime. Each day, two tea pickers are chosen to collect all the lunches, which have been lovingly packed by the women's mothers, sisters or mothers-in-law, and left in bags hanging on trees outside each of their homes. The two women return, arms buckling under the weight of heavy bags stuffed with bottles of drink and parcels of rice and curry.

The tea pickers, who are all women, collect their lunch bags and scatter into small groups. My attention is drawn to one group, who are giggling and affectionately teasing each other. I wander over and start chatting to them while they unwrap their lunch parcels, and am surprised when they pour what appears to be arrack, a strong spirit made from coconuts, into metal cups. One of the women, Mary, offers me some but I decline, explaining that I don't drink alcohol.

'Ha! It's only tea!' she says mischievously, as all the women burst into fits of laughter. 'We keep it in old arrack bottles,' she explains, handing me a cup. It is warm and has the unmistakable bitter–sweet smell of strong black tea laced with sugar.

Mary hands around some *roti*, which goes perfectly with the tea; it is simple but delicious. While we share the *roti*, Mary offers me a taste of her *paruppu* (dhal), which she proudly tells me has been cooked with *elaigova* (a thick spinach) from her garden. She watches my face intently for a reaction, then smiles broadly when I ask for more. The flavours are subtle, with a slight earthiness and are a welcome change to the richer curries I have become accustomed to.

Mary is one of those instantly likeable characters, with a warm personality and generous spirit. She has a profound love for food, and grows her own fruit and veggies on her small plot of land at home. She works three days a week as a tea picker and spends the rest of her time tending to her garden; most of her produce is sold to other tea pickers and anything left over is sold at the local shop.

Full of genuine Sri Lankan hospitality, and pride that comes from cooking your own produce, Mary is quick to invite me to her home for lunch the next day. I am touched by her invitation and can't help but feel a little overwhelmed by the warmth and generosity of the Sri Lankan people.

———————— * ————————

103

Her home is made of mud bricks and is painted a vibrant blue. It is the first in a row of brightly coloured cottages in Carlabeck on Somerset Estate, a 455-hectare tea plantation that is home to 830 tea pickers. Mary lives with her husband, their four daughters and elderly mother-in-law. They are Tamil Christians, unlike most of the other tea pickers on the estate, who are Hindus.

The plot of land behind their home has breathtaking views over the tea fields and mountains. The garden is bursting with avocado, papaya, mango, banana, custard apple, coffee and guava trees, all heavily laden with fruit. There are rows of cabbages and spinach, and a maze of wooden stakes supporting beans, tomatoes and eggplants. The garden produces all the fruit, vegetables and herbs Mary needs for cooking, and she keeps chickens for eggs and goats for milk.

Together we harvest vegetables for lunch and then set to work in the kitchen. This room is the hub of the house; it is rustic and charming, with white-washed walls, a wood-fired stove and a window that looks out onto a massive guava tree.

Mary's mother-in-law, Soosaimary, who is dressed in her best cotton sari for my visit, is keen to lend a watchful eye as Mary shows me how to prepare spinach with dhal (*elaigova vum paruppu*). As we wash and tear the leaves, Mary explains that her husband is a *kangani* (overseer) at the estate and both of them come from a long line of plantation workers. Soosaimary proudly tells me she was a tea picker for thirty-six years.

'This room is the hub of the house; it is rustic and charming, with white-washed walls, a wood-fired stove and a window that looks out onto a massive guava tree.'

Mary gathers some freshly laid eggs from a basket and begins to prepare an intriguing curry. She boils the eggs, peels and fries them whole, then simmers the eggs in a spicy tomato and coconut curry. The aromas are mouthwatering and I have to stop myself from picking up a small spoon to taste it before it's ready.

She then sets to work preparing the *muttagova* (fried cabbage). She stirs mustard and fenugreek seeds, dried chillies, rampe and onions in coconut oil in a blackened wok, then adds some sliced cabbage and turmeric, stirring it over the open fire.

A small wooden table is set in the adjoining room, and we sit down to eat, surrounded by large cooking pots and sacks of rice. We chat happily, Soosaimary and Mary sharing memories of life on the plantation. Their stories are fascinating and the egg curry is utterly delicious.

BOILED EGG CURRY

Serves 4–6 as a side curry

This curry is one of the most memorable dishes I ate in Sri Lanka. It was the first time I had tasted egg curry and it was incredible. The eggs were laid by Mary's hens earlier that morning and, much to my amusement, the hens insisted on being in the kitchen while we were cooking.

INGREDIENTS

6 free-range organic eggs

185 ml (6 fl oz/¾ cup) coconut oil*, plus 1 tablespoon extra

½ red onion*, sliced

2 cloves garlic, ground into a paste

1–2 thin green chillies*, cut into thirds

16 cm (6¼ inch) piece rampe (pandanus) leaf*, cut into 2 cm (¾ inch) pieces

2 small to medium vine-ripened tomatoes, cut into quarters, then small wedges

1 teaspoon Manike's thuna paha (page 153) (or store-bought roasted curry powder)

1 teaspoon ground turmeric

1 teaspoon unroasted chilli powder*

1 teaspoon salt, dissolved in a little warm water

¾ teaspoon black mustard seeds

¾ teaspoon fenugreek seeds

250 ml (9 fl oz/1 cup) coconut cream*

salt, to taste

METHOD

Boil the eggs for 10–12 minutes, or until hard-boiled, then drain and refresh in cold water. Carefully peel the eggs and then prick each egg two or three times with a fork (this allows the flavours of the curry to be absorbed).

Heat the coconut oil in a small wok over medium–high heat and shallow-fry the eggs, spooning them with the oil and turning them over, so both sides are just starting to turn dark golden. Remove with a slotted spoon and drain on paper towel. Drain off the oil left in the wok, then return the wok to the stove.

Heat the extra coconut oil in the wok over medium heat. Add the onion, garlic paste, chillies, rampe and tomatoes. Stir well and cook for 5 minutes, or until the onions have softened. Add the thuna paha, turmeric, chilli powder, salty water, mustard seeds and fenugreek seeds. Mix well and cook for 2 minutes. Add the coconut cream and stir to combine, then add the eggs. Bring almost to the boil, then reduce the heat to low and simmer for 10 minutes, stirring occasionally. Taste and season with salt if needed. Serve with a main curry and with rice or pol roti (page 125).

SPINACH WITH DHAL

Serves 4

To make this dish Mary used a type of spinach called elaigova, *which she picked fresh from her garden. The leaves were quite thick and looked like elephant ears. While I was in Sri Lanka, I ate so many extravagant dishes that I often craved something simple like this. Whenever I asked my hosts for* paruppu *(dhal) and pol roti with nothing else, they found it bizarre, as it's considered 'workers' food' and too simple a dish to be served on its own to a guest — but I loved it.*

INGREDIENTS

250 g (9 oz) English spinach

150 g (5½ oz/¾ cup) chana dhal*, soaked
   in water for 4 hours

¾ teaspoon ground turmeric

1 tablespoon coconut oil*

1 teaspoon salt, dissolved in 60 ml
   (2 fl oz/¼ cup) warm water

2 cloves garlic, ground into a paste

1 red onion*, sliced

2–3 thin green chillies*, cut in half
   on the diagonal

12 cm (4½ inch) piece rampe (pandanus)
   leaf*, cut into 3 cm (1¼ inch) pieces

1 sprig curry leaves, leaves picked

250 ml (9 fl oz/1 cup) coconut cream*

salt, to taste

METHOD

Wash the spinach, then cut the stems into 2 cm (¾ inch) pieces and tear the leaves into smaller pieces.

Drain the soaked dhal, then rinse and drain again. Put the dhal, 500 ml (17 fl oz/2 cups) water and the turmeric in a saucepan and bring to the boil. Cover, reduce the heat to low and simmer for 30–40 minutes, or until the dhal is cooked and the water has been absorbed. Set aside.

Heat the coconut oil in a large wok over medium heat, and add the spinach and salty water. Add the garlic paste, onion, chillies, rampe and curry leaves; cook for 5 minutes, or until the onion has softened. Stir in the dhal and cook for 2 minutes. Pour in the coconut cream and simmer over low heat for 5 minutes, stirring regularly so the coconut cream does not split. Taste and season with salt if needed. Serve with pol roti (page 125).

FRIED CABBAGE

Serves 4–6 as a side dish

Sri Lankans have a gift for turning ordinary ingredients into something quite extraordinary. Cabbage, for example (which I had always considered quite boring), when fried with turmeric, mustard seeds and fresh coconut, is to die for, especially when the cabbage is picked moments before it is cooked and is bursting with flavour. Mary didn't add any freshly scraped coconut to her fried cabbage, as coconuts are not readily available in the area, but try adding a couple of handfuls just before you remove it from the stove.

INGREDIENTS

1 tablespoon coconut oil*

½ red onion*, thinly sliced

2 dried long red chillies*, stalks removed and chopped

8 cm (3¼ inch) piece rampe (pandanus) leaf*, cut into 2 cm (¾ inch) pieces

1 teaspoon black mustard seeds

½ teaspoon fenugreek seeds

600 g (1 lb 5 oz) cabbage, very finely shredded (almost grated)

1 teaspoon ground turmeric

salt, to taste

METHOD

Heat the coconut oil in a large wok over medium heat. Add the onion, dried chillies, rampe, mustard seeds and fenugreek seeds; cook for 3–5 minutes, or until the onions are golden. Add the shredded cabbage and turmeric and stir to combine. Increase the heat to medium–high and cook for 4 minutes, stirring occasionally.

Add 2 tablespoons water, stir well and cook for a further 3 minutes, or until the cabbage is soft. Taste and season with salt if needed. Serve with a main curry.

THE EAST
Rural & Coastal

Vakarai

BATTICALOA

SRI LANKA

Ampara

Pahalalanda

Siyambalanduwa

Monaragala

← Madampe

Buttala

Arugam Bay

Eastern Sri Lanka is home to some of the country's most breathtaking beaches, lagoons and lush tropical countryside. Most areas were previously under the control of the Tamil Tigers (LTTE), but are no longer classified as 'no-go zones' and the opportunity to explore this untapped paradise is luring travellers.

The locals are understandably still tense from the former conflict, but offer travellers some of the country's most heartfelt welcomes. Many towns bear scars from both the tsunami and civil war, and on the surface look like they are still under siege. However, if you are lucky enough to spend a few days with the locals, it is clear that change is taking place and a strong sense of hope and prosperity for the future is emerging.

The people of eastern Sri Lanka are among the poorest in the country, and strive to earn a living through farming and fishing. Despite not being able to afford a wide range of ingredients, they have developed delicious recipes and ingenious cooking methods.

COOKING WITH THE INMATES
Monaragala Prison

I am woken by a series of spine-jarring potholes a few hours into the seven-hour drive from Colombo to Monaragala. The sun is starting to rise, revealing flat green rice paddies that stretch into jungle-clad mountains. We are in the heart of central rural Sri Lanka, in a town called Madampe.

Bleary eyed, I blink twice when I see what looks like a fish market on the side of the road — we are about 100 kilometres from the coast! Rickety wooden tables piled high with fish run for metres along the edge of the road. We stop to stretch our legs and have a look.

As I step out of the car, I am struck by a pungent smell of sweaty seafood and stale ice. Men scurry across the road carrying baskets of fish and ice, which they load into polystyrene boxes strapped onto the back of motorbikes. People raucously barter a purchase price, while men with machetes swiftly scale, gut and chop fish.

I learn from a stallholder called Nimal that most of the fish comes from Tangalle, a town on the south coast, and some from places as far as Negombo, an hour north of Colombo. A typical day for Nimal starts at midnight when he goes to the Tangalle fish markets to buy seafood. He then drives 100 kilometres to Madampe, arriving around 3.30 am to set up his stall. Today's most popular fish is balaya (skipjack tuna) and twenty-two kilograms is bound for Monaragala Prison.

When I visited the prison earlier in the year, to take photographs for the MJF Charitable Foundation, I had the best *pol roti* I have eaten in Sri Lanka. Today I am returning to Monaragala Prison to cook with the inmates and learn the secrets to their amazing *roti*.

When we arrive, we are escorted through the huge grey prison doors and then led to the Senior Superintendent's office. After a cup of tea with the Superintendent and a welfare officer, I am taken through the yard to the kitchen. It is exactly as I remember: a narrow room where the fish is prepared, and alongside, another room with an open fire over which sit massive cooking vats, filled with simmering, aromatic curries.

Outside the kitchen, groups of inmates sit cross-legged on the floor, chopping bunches of leafy green vegetables with strips of tin that look more like prison weapons than kitchen knives. The inmates, although amused by my presence and zealousness, are incredibly welcoming. If it wasn't for the enormous inmate appointed as my bodyguard, I could easily forget that I'm in a prison.

117

Many of the 400 inmates detained in Monaragala Prison are in custody for drug-related offences. Gayan Dissanayake, the prison's welfare officer, explains that because many of the young men are so poor, they are lured into transporting drugs such as marijuana as a means of survival; others are drug addicts. 'Sadly, most of them return to the same community and circumstances upon release and only reoffend,' he says. 'Alcohol abuse is also a major problem in the area, especially in remote villages.'

While stirring a vat of simmering coconut cream and roasted curry powder, a young inmate tells me his story. 'I had too much to drink one night and got into a scuffle. I can't remember exactly what happened.' Stirring in the marinated fish pieces, he adds, 'My family hasn't told anyone I'm here.' The downcast eyes of the other inmates indicate their stories are similar. Not wanting to pry, I divert the conversation towards how to make *pol roti*.

'We only make *pol roti* on special occasions, because flour is expensive,' one of the men explains, as he kneads a mixture of flour, sliced onions, green chillies, curry leaves and water on a large tin lid that serves as a kitchen bench. 'You need lots of freshly scraped coconut for the texture and for the *roti* to break properly. Some people also use coconut water instead of water because it makes it softer.'

He takes a handful of the dough and works it into a small ball, which he then effortlessly moulds into a perfect flat disc. I attempt to follow, but can't seem to get the right shape or thickness. Reverting to a technique used to teach Sri Lankan children how to make *roti*, he demonstrates how I can use the fingers of one hand to flatten the dough on a hard surface, while using the palm of my other hand to guide it into the shape of a circle. Thankfully, I take to this technique fairly quickly.

Making *roti* is not only a treat for me but also the inmates — it is something extra for their lunch. Usually each inmate is restricted to a set portion of rice and curry, which is carefully measured out in tin cups. In all the kitchens I have visited in Sri Lanka, this is the first place I have ever seen anyone measure anything!

Like any prison in the world, Monaragala Prison's doors are constantly revolving. However, with the support of a team of dedicated welfare officers and prison staff, and a helping hand from the MJF Foundation, this is starting to change. A computer lab and woodwork machine donated by the Foundation have enabled the prison staff to set up successful vocational training programmes for the inmates.

Prisoners released on parole are also given assistance by the Foundation in establishing their own businesses through the 'Prison Reform and Reintegrate' initiative of their Small Entrepreneur Programme (SEP). This programme is the first of its kind in Sri Lanka and has had astonishing success. The programme provides eligible prisoners with support in learning a trade, setting up and running their own business. Of the 192 prisoners (at the time of writing) who have taken part in the programme since its inception in 2007, only one participant has reoffended.

I'm interested to learn more, so I ask the Foundation if it's possible for me to visit one of the ex-inmates who has participated in the programme.

BALAYA FISH CURRY

Serves 4

Watching a tough-looking inmate in a torn, dirty singlet hack at a huge balaya fish (skipjack tuna) with a machete wasn't exactly appetising, but this is a delicious recipe and I'm glad I tried it. It has a slight tanginess from the goroka, a sour dried fruit, and a decent kick from the chilli.

INGREDIENTS

4 pieces of goroka*

80 ml (2½ fl oz/⅓ cup) boiled water

500 g (1 lb 2 oz) tuna steaks

185 ml (6 fl oz/¾ cup) coconut cream*

1 red onion*, sliced

1 sprig curry leaves, leaves picked

1 thin green chilli*, halved lengthways

8 cm (3¼ inch) piece rampe (pandanus) leaf*, cut in half

1 teaspoon unroasted chilli powder*

1 teaspoon Manike's thuna paha (page 153) (or store-bought roasted curry powder)

½ teaspoon freshly ground black pepper

1 teaspoon salt

250 ml (9 fl oz/1 cup) coconut milk*

METHOD

Soak the goroka in the boiled water for 30 minutes, then strain, reserving the soaking water. Remove the seeds from the goroka and discard them, then roughly chop. Using a mortar and pestle, pound the goroka into a paste, gradually adding a little of the reserved water. Wash the fish and cut into 3 cm (1¼ inch) cubes, then marinate in the goroka paste and remaining water while you prepare the next step.

In a clay pot or heavy-based saucepan over medium heat, bring the coconut cream to the boil. When the coconut cream releases its oil (a thick cream will float to the surface and form a ring around the edge of the pot), add the onion, curry leaves, chilli, rampe, chilli powder, thuna paha, pepper and salt. Reduce the heat and simmer for 10 minutes, stirring occasionally.

Stir in the coconut milk and bring back to the boil, then reduce the heat and simmer for a further 5–10 minutes, or until the liquid has reduced by about half. Add the marinated fish and simmer gently for 5–8 minutes, or until the fish is just cooked. Serve with pol roti (page 125) and rice.

POL ROTI

Makes 6

Sri Lankan roti is very different from Indian roti; it's much thicker and harder, and usually has freshly scraped coconut (pol) added to the mixture. The best roti I tasted was at Monaragala Prison. The inmates added coconut, green chillies, onions and curry leaves to the mixture. They didn't use any coconut oil, as it's too expensive for prison cooking, but most recipes call for some because it prevents the roti from sticking when you cook it, so I have added a little to their recipe. I have also added bicarbonate of soda, which is used to lighten the texture, although for security reasons it is not allowed in the prison.

INGREDIENTS

180 g (6 oz/1½ cups) freshly scraped
    coconut*

1 red onion*, thinly sliced

4 sprigs curry leaves, leaves picked
    and chopped

4 thin green chillies*, thinly sliced

1 teaspoon salt, dissolved in
    1 tablespoon warm water

1 tablespoon coconut oil*, plus
    2 tablespoons extra

500 g (1 lb 2 oz/3⅓ cups) plain flour

1 teaspoon bicarbonate of soda

METHOD

Place the coconut into a bowl with the onion, curry leaves, chillies, salty water and coconut oil; mix well with your hands. Add the flour and bicarbonate of soda, then mix in 185 ml (6 fl oz/ ¾ cup) water, a little at a time. Knead into a pliable dough.

Work the dough into a large ball, making sure there are no cracks. Rub a little of the extra coconut oil over the dough ball so it doesn't dry out. Take a handful of the dough and roll it into a ball, the size of a tennis ball, smoothing out any cracks. Rub with a little oil. Repeat with the remaining dough to make six balls.

Heat a tava (flat cast-iron roti pan) or a heavy-based frying pan over medium heat. Take a ball of dough and flatten it on a lightly oiled surface (or in your hands) into a disc about 13 cm (5 inches) in diameter and 5 mm (¼ inch) thick. Place the disc of dough on the hot tava and use your fingertips to flatten it a little more, to about 15 cm (6 inches) in diameter. Cook for 3–4 minutes until it starts to colour, then flip it over and cook the other side for a further 3–4 minutes until light golden and crisp. Serve with seeni sambol (page 94), lunu miris (page 61) or any thick curry.

BITTER SWEET
Samantha & Naleeka

This is our first crop,' he proudly explains, as he cuts the pineapple stem with a machete, then breaks the pineapple from its base with his hands. 'We are very excited; we never expected to be growing pineapples.' Sporting an infectious smile and warm eyes, Samantha is the president of a community-based organisation that grows pineapples and oranges in the village of Pahalalanda in Ampara.

An ex-inmate, Samantha has managed to rebuild his life with the help of the MJF Charitable Foundation's Small Entrepreneur Programme (SEP). Samantha served four years in prison for armed robbery, following a drunken night out with some fellow soldiers. 'I thought my life had ended,' he explains. 'I was a soldier who committed this crime; what hope did I have?' In prison he learnt tailoring and when released in 2008, he established his own tailoring business, making uniforms for the Civil Defence troops. 'People started to trust me again. I felt like I was reborn.'

When Samantha's parents arranged for him to meet his future bride, Naleeka, he was surprised to discover she was a woman who had already caught his eye before his fall from grace. Today they live in Pahalalanda, with their six-month-old daughter, in a small mud house opposite a river. His simple but well-equipped tailoring shop is perched on the road in front of their home, with doors that open onto an incredible view of the river and surrounding farmland.

The area was once famous for growing Bibile oranges, a sweet native orange with a thick green skin. The orange farm was abandoned fifty years ago, but in 2010 the Foundation approached the village about recultivating the orchards. A community organisation was formed to initiate the project, named *Gemi Aruna* (meaning 'rebirth' or 'rejuvenation' of the village), and Samantha was appointed as president by the villagers.

On the day the orange seedlings were planted, Samantha's wife discovered she was pregnant, and when their daughter was born she was aptly nicknamed *dodam pelei*, meaning 'orange plant'. 'The orange project not only blessed our family but brought life to the whole village,' Naleeka tells me proudly.

The oranges won't be ready for a few more years but they also planted pineapples, which are faster growing, and today 25,000 are ready to be harvested and sold at the village market. Proudly holding the first pineapple from the crop, Naleeka says, 'I'm making pineapple curry for lunch,' and invites me inside.

Her tiny kitchen is primitive and enchanting; in one corner there's an open fire and a small window next to it, overlooking the garden. She sets to work trimming

127

the pineapple and cutting it into pieces. Placing it in a bowl, she adds slivered garlic and sliced onions, along with fresh curry leaves and rampe from her garden. I am surprised when she reveals that she has never made pineapple curry before. 'I'm creating the recipe as I go,' she says with a smile. A recipe she will no doubt pass on to her daughter.

Naleeka scans jars of spices for inspiration, selecting black mustard seeds, which she sprinkles into a *thaachchiya* (wok) and dry-roasts over the open fire until the seeds crackle and release a nutty aroma. She pounds the seeds into a powder on a heavy stone slab, and mixes the powder with fresh coconut cream. Pouring this over the pineapple and adding more spices, she places it back on the fire. The curry soon takes to the heat, releasing an intoxicating aroma that works havoc on my appetite — thankfully it's not long before it's time to eat.

Chairs are carried outside and we sit in the garden enjoying small bowls of pineapple curry and red rice. The curry exceeds my expectations; I'm not a fan of cooked pineapple, but I am surprised by how delicious it is — it's not too sweet and has a wonderful depth of flavour from the roasted spices.

I am very humbled by their generosity and delighted when Naleeka invites me to dinner at her mother's house, for goat curry, a specialty of the Ampara region.

AMPARA GOAT CURRY

Serves 4 as a side curry

Ampara is famous for mutton, which actually refers to goat in Sri Lanka and not old sheep. As the head of the family, Naleeka's father was responsible for chopping the goat. The liver and heart as well as the bones were added, and although offal is something I usually shy away from, the flavours and aromas from the spices were so delicious I ended up having seconds.

INGREDIENTS

1 kg (2 lb 4 oz) goat (or lamb), preferably leg on the bone

1 teaspoon unroasted chilli powder*

6 green cardamom pods

3 cloves

1 teaspoon Manike's thuna paha (page 153) (or store-bought roasted curry powder)

12 cm (4½ inch) piece rampe (pandanus) leaf*, cut into 4 cm (1½ inch) pieces

1 sprig curry leaves, leaves picked

2 cinnamon sticks, broken into thirds

½ teaspoon freshly ground black pepper

1 teaspoon salt, dissolved in a little warm water

3 cloves garlic, ground into a paste

3 cm (1¼ inch) piece ginger, ground into a paste

2 tablespoons vegetable oil

METHOD

Slice the goat leg through the bone into 2.5 cm (1 inch) thick slices, then cut through the bone into rough 5–6 cm (2–2½ inch) pieces (ask your butcher to do this if you prefer). Set the meat aside.

In a small heavy-based frying pan, dry-roast the chilli powder over low heat for 1 minute, then remove from the pan and place in a large bowl. Dry-roast the cardamom pods and cloves for 2 minutes, then pound into a fine powder using a mortar and pestle (or spice grinder). Transfer to the bowl with the chilli powder, then add the thuna paha, rampe, curry leaves, cinnamon sticks, pepper, salty water, garlic paste and ginger paste; stir to combine. Add the goat pieces and mix well, using your hands to rub the spices into the meat, making sure all the pieces are evenly coated. Set aside at room temperature to marinate for 30 minutes.

Heat the oil in a clay pot or wok over high heat. Add the goat and cook for 3–4 minutes, then turn and cook for a further 3–4 minutes to brown the meat. Add enough water to almost cover the meat (about 750 ml/26 fl oz/3 cups) and bring to the boil. Reduce the heat to low, cover and simmer for 30 minutes, then remove the lid and simmer for a further 1½ hours, stirring occasionally, until the liquid has reduced by half and the meat is tender. Serve with a main curry and rice.

PINEAPPLE CURRY

Serves 4–6 as a side curry

I have never really enjoyed dishes cooked with pineapple, however this curry created by Naleeka, with the first pineapple from their harvest, changed my mind — it was simply delicious. We also ate freshly sliced pineapple sprinkled with black pepper, or chilli powder and salt — bizarre but sensational combinations and wonderfully refreshing in the hot weather.

INGREDIENTS

2 small pineapples (about 1.4 kg/3 lb 2 oz in total), peeled

½ red onion*, sliced

1 sprig curry leaves, leaves picked

12 cm (4½ inch) piece rampe (pandanus) leaf*, cut into 3 cm (1¼ inch) pieces

1 clove garlic, finely chopped

1 teaspoon black mustard seeds

125 ml (4 fl oz/½ cup) coconut cream*

1 teaspoon unroasted chilli powder*

¼ teaspoon ground turmeric

1 teaspoon Manike's thuna paha (page 153) (or store-bought roasted curry powder)

250 ml (9 fl oz/1 cup) coconut milk*

salt, to taste

METHOD

Cut each pineapple into quarters lengthways. Slice the pineapple into 2 cm (¾ inch) thick pieces and put in a bowl. Add the onion, curry leaves, rampe and garlic and set aside.

In a small heavy-based frying pan, dry-roast the mustard seeds over medium heat for about 2–3 minutes, or until fragrant. Cool slightly, then using a mortar and pestle, pound the seeds into a fine powder. Combine with the coconut cream and set aside.

Dry-roast the chilli powder over medium heat for 2–3 minutes, or until fragrant and darker in colour. Add to the pineapple, along with the turmeric and thuna paha; mix to combine. Transfer to a wok and pour in the coconut milk. Cook over medium heat for 15 minutes, or until the pineapple is tender, stirring regularly. Add the coconut cream and mustard and simmer for a further 3 minutes, stirring continuously so the coconut cream does not split. Season to taste with salt. Serve with a main curry and rice.

A SWEETER LIFE
Sumith

Make sure you bring me back some milk toffee,' says my friend Sumithra when she finds out I'm going to Hulandawa, near Monaragala. I discovered Sumith's milk toffee on my previous visit to Sri Lanka, and despite having visited more kitchens than tourist sights, I still haven't found anyone who can make better milk toffee than Sumith. I'm not sure why his tastes so good, but it does. And this time I'm back to learn his secret.

Sumith, a humble and softly spoken man, greets me with '*ayubowan*', meaning 'welcome' in Sinhala, as he opens the doors to his factory at the back of his house. It is like travelling back in time: wood fires heat vats of milk and sugar for the toffee; on a nearby table, glass bottles are used to roll out dough for the chilli bites, which are then cut into crescent shapes using old bottle tops.

Sumith's short plump wife, Rohini, walks in, balancing a tray of steaming milky tea in one hand and a plate of milk toffee in the other. Smiling warmly, she signals for me to take a seat at the wooden table where a group of women are rolling out dough. The women welcome me with their dark eyes and a gentle bow of their heads. As they continue to roll out the dough, they chat softly to one another, gliding through their work with quiet purpose.

I take a sip of the sweet milky tea and slide a square of toffee into my mouth. It dissolves, releasing a buttery caramel flavour, with a hint of vanilla and an unmistakable soft smokiness from being cooked over an open fire. I reach for another piece and politely mutter '*rasai isthuti*', meaning 'delicious, thank you'. Before I can finish what's in my mouth, Rohini offers me the plate again. '*Thawa chuttak*? A little more?' How can I refuse? After all, this is her recipe … well, her mother's to be exact.

Sumith initially started a yoghurt manufacturing business from his home kitchen. However, in 1998, after its first year of operation, business became slow due to an outbreak of cholera, which contaminated the town's milk supply. He needed a recipe that used boiled milk to remove the impurities. Rohini suggested her mother's milk toffee and taught him how to make it.

Through an open doorway that leads into the back of the factory, I can see a young woman dressed in pale blue, sitting by a massive vat over a fire. Glistening with sweat, she is unfazed by the heat, gently stirring the vat with a huge wooden paddle. I wander over and discover she is boiling milk for the next batch of toffee.

Next to her, a woman is crouched over a *thaachchiya* (wok), tending to a batch of toffee that is just starting to caramelise. I am mesmerised by the way she rhythmically

137

swirls the thickening mixture, my gaze only lifting when she removes the toffee from the fire to stir in the vanilla essence. The heat immediately intensifies the vanilla aroma — it's heavenly.

Not surprisingly, milk toffee is one of Sumith's best-selling products and at 5 rupees a square, it is affordable. The secret, Sumith tells me, 'is to use good-quality fresh milk; we don't compromise'. In fact, he pays his milk suppliers 5 rupees more per litre than the normal market price to guarantee the quality.

With his enterprising spirit and determination, it is no surprise Sumith caught the attention of the MJF Charitable Foundation. A few years ago, as part of their Small Entrepreneur Programme (SEP), a unique initiative that assists individuals establish their own business, the Foundation helped Sumith buy a three-wheeler so he no longer had to rely on the sporadic local bus service to make his deliveries. The Foundation gave him 50,000 rupees to make the first payment and he paid the remainder in monthly instalments. He proudly tells me, 'I paid it all off last year.' As we chat, I discover there are some interesting conditions to the Foundation's assistance. Sumith is required to save 10,000 rupees per month to go towards developing his business. He also has to find someone deserving in the community and assist them in a similar way to how the Foundation has helped him.

Out of the dozen workers at Sumith's factory, there is one woman whose infectious smile and bubbly personality has caught my attention; her name is Pushpadevi. As she rolls out the dough for the chilli bites, she tells me her story. She is Tamil and comes from Buttala, a neighbouring village. She was married at eighteen, and has two young children, but towards the end of the war her husband went missing and she has not seen him since. 'I did everything I could to find him. I don't know whether to keep hoping or give up,' she quietly says. While this is painful for Pushpadevi, she has learnt to cope as best she can. Getting up, she brushes the flour off her hands. 'Come, it's time to fry the chilli bites.'

The others have already made a head start in the back room and a gigantic *thaachchiya* is bubbling with hot oil. The oil spits and hisses as one of the women drops a huge bundle of crescent dough pieces into the oil. Within seconds, they puff up and expand, turning a rich golden yellow. She drains the pastry puffs and lays them out on a piece of torn cardboard. When they have cooled a little, she coats them in a frightening amount of salt and chilli, and a little *ajinomoto*. Offering me some, I almost choke on the fumes of chilli. Cautiously I pop a couple into my mouth. It's an explosion of tastes and textures: crisp and crunchy, with a salty, spicy kick that leaves me wanting more.

While Sumith bundles up a bag of chilli bites for me, we chat about his plans for the future. A true entrepreneur, Sumith is intent on expanding his business. 'If I can save 2 million rupees by next year, I can buy another lorry and some machinery to heat the milk, as well as employ fifteen more staff.' While I admire Sumith's determination and spirit, I hope his humble factory doesn't change too much.

CHILLI BITES

Serves 8–10

Sumith's chilli bites are dangerously addictive. So much so that the day before I was due to fly home, I rang Sumith and ordered two kilos of them. Unfazed by my request, he bundled them up and put them on the next bus bound for Colombo. Eighteen hours later I was munching on chilli bites as I boarded the plane.

INGREDIENTS

635 g (1 lb 6½ oz/4¼ cups) plain flour

½ teaspoon dried yeast

1½ cloves garlic, finely chopped

⅛ teaspoon sugar

⅛ teaspoon egg yellow powdered food colouring*

750 ml (26 fl oz/3 cups) coconut oil* or vegetable oil, for deep-frying

1 teaspoon unroasted chilli powder*

1 teaspoon salt

1 teaspoon ajinomoto* (optional)

METHOD

In a large bowl, combine the flour, yeast, garlic and sugar. Mix the food colouring with 310 ml (10¾ fl oz/1¼ cups) water, then add to the flour mixture and mix well. Add a little extra water, if needed, to bring the dough together. Cover the bowl with plastic wrap and leave the dough to rise in a warm place for 2 hours.

Once the dough has risen, roll it out on a lightly floured surface to a 2 mm (1/16 inch) thickness. Using a bottle top, cut out small crescent moon shapes. Heat the oil in a wok or large saucepan to approximately 170°C (325°F) (a cube of bread dropped into the oil will brown in 20 seconds). Deep-fry the dough pieces in batches for 3 minutes, or until puffy, light golden and crisp. Remove with a slotted spoon, drain on paper towel and cool.

In a large zip-lock plastic bag, put the chilli powder, salt and ajinomoto (if you aren't using ajinomoto, add an extra 1 teaspoon salt), and shake to combine. Add the fried dough pieces and shake well until they are evenly coated in the chilli mix.

SUMITH'S MILK TOFFEE

Makes 24 squares

Sri Lankans have a real sweet tooth and milk toffee is very popular. Sumith's was, without a doubt, the best I tasted and it should probably come with a warning on the packet that you won't be able to stop at just one piece. I bought a couple of bags as a present for a friend in Colombo, but on the long drive back they somehow managed to disappear!

INGREDIENTS

1 litre (35 fl oz/4 cups) full-cream milk

600 g (1 lb 5 oz/2⅔ cups) caster sugar

a few drops of vanilla essence

METHOD

Lightly grease a 16 x 26 cm (6¼ x 10½ inch) shallow baking tin and line the base and sides with non-stick baking paper, leaving some excess paper hanging over the sides of the tin.

Heat the milk and sugar in a heavy-based saucepan over medium heat, stirring continuously until it comes to the boil. Reduce the heat to low and simmer gently, stirring occasionally, for about 30–40 minutes, or until the mixture starts to thicken and caramelise. Simmer for a further 10–20 minutes, stirring constantly. To check if the toffee is ready, use a teaspoon to pour a few drops of toffee into a cup of water and then take the toffee out and roll it between your fingers — the toffee should form a small soft ball and not stick to your fingers.

When the toffee is cooked, remove the pan from the heat and stir in the vanilla. Pour into the prepared tin, then place another piece of lightly greased baking paper on top. Allow to cool slightly (the toffee needs to be set but still slightly pliable so you can cut it).

Remove from the tin, place on a chopping board and remove the top layer of paper. Using a small, lightly greased serrated knife, cut the toffee into 3 cm (1¼ inch) squares, then leave to cool.

LASTING IMPRESSIONS
Manike

'Just close your eyes and tip the water quickly,' Manike says encouragingly. Trying not to think about how murky it is, I do as she says and, with a little too much gusto, dump the bucket of water over myself, losing my footing and nearly my sarong. Manike cannot help but giggle as I attempt to retrieve my dignity. It never occurred to me that bathing by a well would be so difficult!

An invitation to stay with Manike's family, who live in a remote rural village, came as I was nearing the end of my month-long trip in Sri Lanka. Tired of staying in hotels, I jumped at the chance; this was the authentic experience I was craving. They live in a mud hut in a village called Siyambalanduwa, one of the poorest in eastern Sri Lanka, and predominately a Sinhalese Buddhist farming community.

It is almost dark by the time we finish bathing and make our way back up the path to Manike's mud hut, which is nestled among papaya, jackfruit, coconut and pomegranate trees. I follow Manike into the kitchen. It is the colour and texture of earth; it's dark but inviting and filled with all the essentials: an oil lamp, wood-fired stove, clay pots, stone slab for grinding spices, bags of rice, an array of spices, a mound of coconuts and a small number of cups and plates.

Manike is a small, strong woman with weathered hands and a mischievous smile. Lighting an oil lamp, she tells me, 'We used to have solar power, but it's not working and we can't afford to repair it.' It has been a tough year she explains; they were forced to sell their only bull to secure a new plot of land to grow their vegetables on. 'We worked twenty days straight to clear the jungle before we could plant anything,' says Manike, who worked alongside her husband.

Manike's seventeen-year-old daughter, Jeevamali, appears in the doorway, balancing two jugs of water on her hips; it is her job to collect the evening's water. She sets the water down on the table and then goes off to study and, while we wash the vegetables, Manike and I chat about her hopes for her daughters' futures.

Jeevamali wants to go to university and become a doctor. Manike's eldest daughter, Nimali, is nineteen and lives with her aunt, who is teaching her to sew; they are anxious to find her a 'good Buddhist husband'. Manike and her husband have a small plot of land with coconuts growing on it, which they plan to give to their daughter as a dowry. Sachini, her second youngest, is eleven and is determined to become an art teacher. 'She spends hours each night painting while Jeevamali studies,' says Manike. Her youngest, Vihangi, is seven and she enjoys helping in the kitchen.

147

Manike could talk all night about her daughters, but she is anxious to get dinner ready. Slicing the eggplant (*brinjal*), she tosses them in turmeric and salt. 'I hope you like *brinjal moju*,' she asks, casting me a cheeky smile. I had arrived at Manike's with a bag of *brinjals* and a pleading request to learn how to make *brinjal moju*, a caramelised eggplant pickle, which I adore. 'The trick is to balance the sweet and sour flavours,' says Manike, as she reaches for a clay pot from the shelf.

With the *brinjal moju* well under way, Manike's husband, Indrawansa, strolls in, covered in beads of sweat, his arms laden with okra (ladies fingers) and pumpkin. Conversation soon turns to how the crop is coming along. 'The corn should be ready next month, as long as the rats stay away,' he explains. Over the next month or so, Indrawansa will spend his nights in a hut in the middle of his field, keeping watch over the corn to make sure the animals don't destroy it.

'I'll visit each day to bring him food,' Manike says. Knowing their plot of land is a two-hour bike ride away, I can't imagine how Manike has time to do this, as well as tend to her chores, look after the children and milk the cows.

Soon the kitchen bench is strewn with an array of delicious-looking dishes: the *brinjal moju*, okra curry, pumpkin curry, *paruppu* (dhal), *gotu kola* (Sri Lankan tabouli), pappadum pieces and red rice. Manike piles my plate high until she is satisfied it can't hold any more, then serves her husband and continues to busy

herself in the kitchen. I negotiate my way through the mound of curries on my plate, the flavours melding surprisingly well together. Once we have all eaten, Manike serves herself and sits down.

No sooner has she started to eat than there is a knock at the door; it's one of the local farmers, who has damaged his eye in an accident in the field. Manike is the local medicine woman and has cured many of the villagers with Ayurvedic remedies that she learnt from her father. Most of Manike's remedies come from plants grown in her garden. She doesn't charge for her treatments, believing her knowledge is a gift that should be shared freely.

As the evening draws to a close, it is time for bed. Jeevamali kindly gives me her tiny room. Exhausted, I flop onto the bed, but my body thuds as it hits the mattress. Lifting the thin sheet, I discover the bed is merely a plank of wood. I'm worried I might be in for a sleepless night, but I'm exhausted and quickly drift off to sleep.

> *'Manike is the local medicine woman and has cured many of the villagers with Ayurvedic remedies that she learnt from her father.'*

It is 4 am when Manike wakes me, holding an oil lamp in one hand and a hot cup of tea in the other. Stumbling out of bed, I find Jeevamali busy ironing the school uniforms with a heavy, cast-iron flat iron, heated with burnt-down coconut shells. When the ironing is finished, she sits down to cram in some study before the sun rises; she then collects the water and sweeps the house.

After the girls leave for school, Manike finally sits down. Over a breakfast of *roti* and leftover pumpkin curry, we map out our day. There is washing to do and today is also market day. But first, Manike is going to show me how to make *piti guli*, a Sri Lankan version of a doughnut. 'It's a traditional recipe from this village,' she explains proudly. 'You won't find it in other areas. It is my husband's favourite.'

Working the simple flour, bicarb soda and water mixture into a sticky dough, Manike tells me that we should let the dough rest for an hour first, but today we are pressed for time, so she adds the sugar and salt, and continues to twist and pull the dough. When it has the right elastic consistency, she takes a handful, clenches her fist and squeezes out a ball of dough, which she drops into boiling coconut oil. I have a go, but getting the right shape turns out to be harder than it looks and Manike is quick to rescue the remaining mixture.

As we share some *piti guli* and a cup of spicy coffee made with freshly roasted coffee beans from her garden, Manike tells me how she will be sad when it is time for me to leave. 'I will feel like I'm losing a daughter,' she quietly says. 'But perhaps you can come back again in April, when the coffee bush has ripened? I can teach you my father's recipe for coffee.'

Her offer is too good to refuse and I immediately agree. Planning my return visit, I ask if there is anything I can bring back for her. Manike, who rarely asks for anything, strangely replies, 'Yes, please. Some bras.'

MANIKE'S THUNA PAHA

Makes 120 g (4¼ oz/1 cup)

Thuna paha *means 'three by five' in Sinhala and is a spice mix found in most Sri Lankan kitchens. Each family has their own special blend — I have eaten the same curry in different homes across the island, yet each was slightly different. Manike makes hers the traditional way, where the spices are left to dry in the sun for a day and then ground on a heavy stone slab. The spice mix can be used when making just about any curry.*

INGREDIENTS

50 g (1¾ oz/heaped ½ cup) coriander seeds

25 g (1 oz/2½ tablespoons) cumin seeds

25 g (1 oz/2½ tablespoons) fennel seeds

6 cm (2½ inch) piece rampe (pandanus) leaf*

1 sprig curry leaves, including the stem

1 cinnamon stick, broken into pieces

METHOD

Put the coriander, cumin and fennel seeds in a shallow tray or dish. Place the rampe leaf and curry leaves in another tray or dish. Leave to dry in the sun for a day. When dried, break the rampe into 2 cm (¾ inch) pieces. Pick the curry leaves off the stems and cut the stems into 1 cm (½ inch) pieces.

In a small wok or heavy-based frying pan, dry-roast the coriander, cumin and fennel seeds over very high heat for 3–5 minutes, or until fragrant, tossing them continuously. Add the rampe pieces, curry leaves, chopped stems and cinnamon stick. Immediately remove the wok from the heat, but keep stirring so the curry leaves become roasted from the residual heat contained in the spices.

Set aside to cool. Using a mortar and pestle (or spice grinder), pound the spices into a fine powder. Store in an airtight container for up to 2 months.

POLOS AMBULA

Serves 6

Manike cooked this curry with fresh polos from her garden. To cut them, she wedged a knife between her toes, with the blade facing upwards, then sliced the polos on the upturned blade. This is the traditional way women in the villages cut veggies — it looks dangerous but they have it down to a fine art. Another key ingredient in this dish is goroka, a dried sour fruit, and this is where the dish gets its name: ambula means 'sour' in Sinhala and polos means 'young green jackfruit'. The curry is best cooked in a clay pot and the flavours are enhanced if left overnight.

INGREDIENTS

2 teaspoons ground turmeric, plus 1 teaspoon extra

1 young green jackfruit (polos)* or 2 tins (560 g/1 lb 4 oz each) young green jackfruit in brine, drained and rinsed

10 small pink Asian shallots*, thinly sliced

1 clove garlic, finely chopped

1 sprig curry leaves, leaves picked

2 teaspoons Manike's thuna paha (page 153) (or store-bought roasted curry powder)

1 teaspoon unroasted chilli powder*

½ teaspoon fenugreek seeds

1 teaspoon salt

1 goroka*

500 ml (17 fl oz/2 cups) coconut milk*

185 ml (6 fl oz/¾ cup) coconut cream*

METHOD

Fill a large bowl with water, sprinkle in the turmeric and stir to combine. Set aside. If using fresh young jackfruit, rub your hands with oil to protect them, as the jackfruit releases a sticky gum when cut. Cut the jackfruit in half and then into quarters. Take a small amount of the sticky gum in your fingertips, roll it into a ball and use this to collect the rest of the gum off the fruit. Then, using a piece of paper, rub off any residue. Cut off the skin from each piece. Cut off the centre core and discard it, then cut into 2–2.5 cm (¾–1 inch) thick pieces. To prevent further discolouring, submerge the jackfruit pieces into the bowl of turmeric water, stir with your hands and leave for 2 minutes before draining.

In a clay pot or heavy-based saucepan, put the jackfruit, shallots, garlic, curry leaves, thuna paha, chilli powder, extra turmeric, fenugreek seeds, salt and goroka. Add the coconut milk, coconut cream and 60 ml (2 fl oz/¼ cup) water (or enough to cover all the ingredients). Bring to the boil, then reduce the heat to low–medium and simmer for 30–45 minutes, stirring occasionally, until the curry starts to thicken. Cover and simmer over low heat for a further 30–45 minutes, or until most of the coconut milk has evaporated. Remove from the heat, then extract the goroka and discard it. Serve with rice.

FRIED POTATO

Serves 4 as a side dish

Most curries in Sri Lanka include coconut milk or coconut cream, but this is one dish that doesn't. It's simple to make and is a perfect side dish to any curry. For those who don't like too much heat, you might want to reduce the chilli, as it has quite a fiery kick!

INGREDIENTS

500 g (1 lb 2 oz) waxy potatoes, peeled and cut into 2 cm (¾ inch) cubes
1 red onion*, sliced
1 sprig curry leaves, leaves picked
1 teaspoon ground turmeric
½ teaspoon Manike's thuna paha (page 153) (or store-bought roasted curry powder)

¼ teaspoon freshly ground black pepper
1 teaspoon salt
2 tablespoons coconut oil*
2 teaspoons dried chilli pieces*

METHOD

Put the potatoes, onion, curry leaves, turmeric, thuna paha, pepper and salt into a bowl and mix, making sure the potato is evenly coated in the spices.

Heat the coconut oil in a wok over high heat. Add the dried chilli pieces and potato mixture and fry for 2 minutes, then reduce the heat, cover and cook for 20 minutes, or until the potatoes are tender, turning them occasionally so they don't stick to the bottom of the wok (take care when turning the potatoes so they don't break up). When the potatoes are golden and cooked through, transfer to a bowl. Serve with a main curry and rice.

BRINJAL MOJU

Serves 4 as a side dish

This fried eggplant pickle was the dish that first sparked my love for Sri Lankan cuisine. The first time I tasted brinjal moju was at a roadside eatery in the remote village of Mankada. It was unlike anything I had ever eaten: the subtle tanginess from the coconut vinegar and the slight sweetness from the sugar and fried eggplant worked brilliantly together. This is the recipe Manike shared with me.

INGREDIENTS

6 long, thin light purple eggplants (brinjal)

1 teaspoon ground turmeric, plus
    ½ teaspoon extra

salt

2 sprigs curry leaves, leaves picked
    and roughly chopped

500 ml (17 fl oz/2 cups) coconut oil*,
    for deep-frying

6 small pink Asian shallots*, thinly sliced

3 thin green chillies*, cut into thirds

1 teaspoon black mustard seeds, ground
    using a mortar and pestle

1 clove garlic, ground into a paste

1 teaspoon unroasted chilli powder*

2 teaspoons sugar

1 tablespoon coconut vinegar*
    (or rice vinegar)

80 ml (2½ fl oz/⅓ cup) coconut cream*

METHOD

Slice the eggplants in half and then into quarters lengthways. Place the eggplants in a bowl with the turmeric and 1 teaspoon salt; toss to coat well. Add the curry leaves and set aside.

Heat the coconut oil in a small wok to approximately 160°C (315°F) (a cube of bread dropped into the oil will brown in 30 seconds). Mix the shallots with a pinch of salt, then deep-fry the shallots for 3 minutes, or until dark golden brown. Remove with a slotted spoon and drain on paper towel. Deep-fry the chillies for 1–2 minutes, or until golden brown. Remove and drain on paper towel. Deep-fry the eggplant and curry leaves in two batches for 3–4 minutes, or until golden brown, being careful not to overcook them. Remove and drain on paper towel.

In a heavy-based saucepan or clay pot, combine the fried eggplants, shallots and chillies. Add the ground mustard seeds, garlic paste, chilli powder, extra turmeric, 1 teaspoon salt, sugar, coconut vinegar and coconut cream. Cover and cook over low heat for 5 minutes, or until the coconut cream has evaporated. Serve with a main curry and rice.

OKRA CURRY

Serves 6 as a side curry

Manike cooked this dish with fresh okra (referred to as ladies fingers in Sri Lanka) and plump juicy cherry tomatoes, which were grown on their plot of land. I love the freshness and simplicity of this dish; the flavours are delicate and it's not too heavily spiced. Although she served it as a side curry, I could have easily devoured an entire bowl on its own.

INGREDIENTS

380 g (13½ oz/about 20) large okra (ladies fingers), about 10 cm (4 inches) long

16 cherry tomatoes, sliced in half

6 small pink Asian shallots*, sliced

2–3 thin green chillies*, cut into thirds

2 sprigs curry leaves, leaves picked

2 teaspoons ground turmeric

2 teaspoons Manike's thuna paha (page 153) (or store-bought roasted curry powder)

2 teaspoons salt

2 tablespoons coconut oil*

125 ml (4 fl oz/½ cup) coconut milk*

METHOD

Cut the ends off the okra and discard them, then slice each okra on the diagonal into three pieces. Place in a bowl with the tomatoes, shallots, chillies, curry leaves, turmeric, thuna paha and salt. Mix well to evenly coat the okra pieces in the spices.

Heat the coconut oil in a clay pot or heavy-based saucepan over medium heat. Add the okra mixture and cook for 5 minutes. Add the coconut milk, then cover, reduce the heat to low and cook for a further 10 minutes, or until the okra are tender. Serve with a main curry and rice.

PUMPKIN CURRY
Serves 4–6

This thick, creamy curry, made with tender chunks of pumpkin, is enhanced by a burst of flavour from tempered onions, curry leaves and mustard seeds. Tempering is a method used often in Sri Lankan cooking and is a great way to increase the flavours of a curry. The technique involves frying onions, mustard seeds, sometimes fenugreek or cumin seeds, and curry leaves in oil until they are brown, slightly crisp and aromatic. This mixture is added to the curry just before it is served.

CURRY

750 g (1 lb 10 oz) Jap pumpkin, seeded and cut into 5–6 cm (2–2½ inch) pieces (skin left on)

4 small pink Asian shallots*, sliced

2 thin green chillies*, cut into thirds

1 sprig curry leaves, leaves picked and roughly chopped

8 cm (3¼ inch) piece rampe (pandanus) leaf*, cut into 2 cm (¾ inch) pieces

1 teaspoon unroasted chilli powder*

1 teaspoon ground turmeric

½ teaspoon fenugreek seeds

1½ teaspoons Manike's thuna paha (page 153) (or store-bought roasted curry powder)

1 teaspoon salt

500 ml (17 fl oz/2 cups) coconut milk*

250 ml (9 fl oz/1 cup) coconut cream*

FOR TEMPERING

2 tablespoons coconut oil*

1 teaspoon black mustard seeds

2 small pink Asian shallots*, sliced

1 sprig curry leaves, leaves picked

METHOD

To make the curry, place the pumpkin into a clay pot or heavy-based saucepan, add the rest of the curry ingredients and mix to combine. There should be just enough coconut milk and cream to cover the pumpkin pieces.

Bring to the boil, then cover, reduce the heat to low and simmer for 10–12 minutes, or until the pumpkin is tender, stirring the curry occasionally so the coconut milk does not split. Remove from the heat and set aside.

For tempering, heat the coconut oil in a small wok or frying pan over medium heat and add the mustard seeds. When the seeds start to pop, add the shallots and curry leaves and cook for 3–5 minutes, or until the shallots are dark brown and starting to crisp a little. Remove from the heat and strain through a sieve. Stir half of the tempered mixture into the curry and garnish with the remaining mixture. Serve with pol roti (page 125) and rice.

SMASHING EGGPLANT CURRY

Serves 4 as a side curry

This dish is known as thalana batu, *named after the main ingredient in the curry, the slightly bitter, small, white–green eggplants. I first came across them at the Siyambalanduwa markets. Intrigued, I took some back to Manike and asked how to prepare them. It was a little fiddly to remove their seeds, but lots of fun bashing the eggplants to split them open. This curry has loads of flavour and is quite unique, with a slight bitterness from the eggplants, strong turmeric overtones and a stunning creamy texture. It is best served as a side dish, as it's quite rich.*

INGREDIENTS

40 g (1½ oz/1 tablespoon) tamarind pulp*, soaked in 125 ml (4 fl oz/½ cup) warm water

600 g (1 lb 5 oz/about 20) Thai (apple) eggplants

4 small pink Asian shallots*, thinly sliced

1 thin green chilli*, cut into thirds (optional)

½ sprig curry leaves, leaves picked

1 teaspoon ground turmeric

½ teaspoon Manike's thuna paha (page 153) (or store-bought roasted curry powder)

½ teaspoon unroasted chilli powder*

salt

1 tablespoon coconut oil*

125 ml (4 fl oz/½ cup) coconut cream*

METHOD

Prepare the tamarind pulp following the method on page 261. Set the tamarind water aside.

Put the eggplants into a plastic bag and place on a chopping board. Smash the eggplants with the base of a heavy-based saucepan, making sure each one bursts open. Remove the eggplants from the bag and place in a bowl of salty water; this will stop them from browning. Use your fingers to scoop out the seeds from each eggplant (the seeds are very bitter), break off the stem and discard it, then return the eggplant to the water. Drain the eggplants and rinse well to remove the excess seeds.

Place the eggplants in a large bowl and combine with the shallots, chilli, curry leaves, turmeric, thuna paha, chilli powder and 1 teaspoon salt; mix well.

Heat the coconut oil in a clay pot or heavy-based saucepan over medium–high heat. Add the eggplant mixture and cook for 4 minutes, stirring regularly, then add the tamarind water and cook for 1 minute. Add the coconut cream, then cover, reduce the heat to low and simmer for 20 minutes, or until the eggplants are tender. Serve with a main curry and rice.

GOTU KOLA
Serves 6–8

Gotu kola is the Sri Lankan version of Middle Eastern tabouli, and is a refreshing accompaniment to curries. I love fresh salad, but Sri Lankans don't eat salads that often. When I discovered gotu kola I ate it almost every day. If you are unable to get gotu kola, substitute it with flat-leaf parsley. The fresh coconut, sprats (dried baby fish) and lime juice give this salad a typical Sri Lankan flavour.

INGREDIENTS

260 g (9¼ oz) gotu kola* (or flat-leaf parsley), stems removed

¾ tablespoon sprats* (dried baby fish)

60 g (2¼ oz/½ cup) freshly scraped coconut*

1–2 thin green chillies*, finely chopped

4 small pink Asian shallots*, very finely chopped

juice of 1 lime

½ teaspoon salt

METHOD

Wash the gotu kola (or parsley) leaves in cold water, then dry them and chop finely. In a small heavy-based frying pan, dry-roast the sprats for 3–4 minutes until golden brown and crisp. Remove from the heat and allow to cool. Using a mortar and pestle (or spice grinder), pound the sprats into a coarse powder.

In a small bowl, combine the ground sprats with the coconut, chillies, shallots, lime juice and salt. Add the gotu kola and mix all the ingredients together. Serve with a curry and rice.

SPICY SRI LANKAN COFFEE

Serves 4

When I stayed with Manike and her family, I was surprised to find a coffee bush in their garden. Making kopi *(coffee) the traditional way is incredibly labour-intensive. The ripe coffee beans are picked and left in the sun to dry for four days, then pounded in a huge mortar and pestle to remove the tough outer shells. The inner beans are then roasted in a wok over an open fire. Coriander seeds and black peppercorns are added at the end, releasing an incredible aroma, and these give the coffee its unique flavour and a bit of a kick! The beans are then pounded by hand into ground coffee. Sri Lankans drink their coffee black and strong, with lots of sugar. This recipe for Manike's father's* kopi *has been simplified, so it is more realistic to make at home, but if you want to try roasting your own beans, see the note below.*

INGREDIENTS

2 teaspoons coriander seeds

½ teaspoon black peppercorns

30 g (1 oz/4 scoops) of freshly ground
   coffee

500 ml (17 fl oz/2 cups) boiling water

3 tablespoons sugar

METHOD

In a small wok or heavy-based frying pan, dry-roast the coriander seeds and peppercorns over low heat for 3–5 minutes, or until fragrant. Cool slightly, then using a mortar and pestle (or spice grinder), pound the spices into a fine powder.

Place the spices in a large coffee plunger, with the freshly ground coffee, and pour in the boiling water. Infuse for 5 minutes, then plunge and pour into four espresso cups. Add 3 teaspoons of sugar to each, stir well and serve.

NOTE: It's surprisingly easy to roast your own coffee beans at home. Green coffee beans are available from coffee roasters. Dry-fry them in a small wok or heavy-based frying pan for 5–10 minutes over medium–high heat, stirring regularly, until the beans start to pop, smoke and turn medium dark brown. Remove the wok from the heat before the beans get too dark (they will retain heat and continue to cook), then add the spices. Knowing exactly when to remove the beans from the heat takes a little bit of practice, as it's hard to see the colour change because of all the smoke. Cool before grinding in a coffee grinder or spice grinder. For best results, allow the roasted coffee beans to rest for 12–24 hours before grinding.

PITI GULI

Makes about 10

These sweet fried balls of dough are a bit like doughnuts, and are a traditional recipe from Siyambalanduwa. Piti means flour in Sinhala and guli refers to the ball-like shape. The ingredients are really simple — so simple in fact that I didn't expect them to be so tasty — and frying the dough in coconut oil adds a delicious and distinct flavour. The trick to getting the dough right is in the twisting and stretching, which takes a little practice.

INGREDIENTS

300 g (10½ oz/2 cups) plain flour

2 teaspoons bicarbonate of soda

55 g (2 oz/¼ cup) caster sugar

pinch of salt

750 ml (26 fl oz/3 cups) coconut oil*

METHOD

Sift the flour and bicarbonate of soda into a bowl. Using a wooden spoon, gradually mix in 185 ml (6 fl oz/¾ cup) water, a little at a time, working the mixture into a wet, sticky dough. Set aside for about 1 hour for the gluten to settle. Knead in the sugar and a pinch of salt. Continue to knead and stretch the dough for 6–8 minutes, or until it is sticky and elastic.

Heat the coconut oil in a wok or heavy-based saucepan to approximately 180°C (350°F) (a cube of bread dropped into the oil will brown in 15 seconds). Take a level tablespoon of the sticky dough and, using another spoon, slowly scrape the batter off the spoon into the hot oil. Deep-fry for 2 minutes, then turn it over and fry for a further 2 minutes, or until golden brown. Remove with a slotted spoon and place in a colander to drain. Repeat with the remaining sticky dough, frying in batches of three at a time. Serve warm or cold with a cup of spicy Sri Lankan coffee (page 173).

COOKING WITH THE ARMY
233 Brigade, Vakarai

When I wake it takes me a few moments to remember where I am. Pushing my mosquito net aside, I watch the sun rise over the lagoon from my bed. Everything is completely still; the only sign of life, a silhouetted fisherman in a wooden canoe that silently glides past. I take it all in, determined to cement this moment to memory.

It is not every day that I wake up in an army camp in a foreign country. I'm in Vakarai, a small town about 60 kilometres north of Batticaloa — formerly a Tamil Tiger (LTTE) stronghold — with the 233 Brigade. Breathtakingly beautiful and serene, it's hard to imagine that it was here, only a few years ago, that one of the bloodiest battles between the Sri Lankan Army and the Tamil Tigers took place. Strangely, the army runs a cashew nut nursery and I have come to Vakarai Camp to visit the nursery and learn how to cook cashew curry.

On the edge of the lagoon is a beaten-up tin shed that functions as one of the mess kitchens. I walk across the camp, nervously trying to avoid over a dozen barking dogs, and I'm greeted at the door by General Wickramasinghe, his massive smile instantly putting me at ease. Inside it is spacious and airy, with large windows, corrugated-iron walls, a cabinet filled with mismatched old china, and a large gas burner. This is where the general's and other high-ranking officers' meals are prepared.

The cook tells me the secret to making a good cashew curry is to use superior quality *cadjus* (cashews). He can't stop grinning, clearly amused by my request to cook with him. A crowd of soldiers soon gathers in the kitchen. I decide to take some photographs and without thinking, fling open my light diffuser, which makes a loud popping sound. The soldiers jump to attention, grabbing their AK47s, and circle me. When they realise my diffuser is not a weapon, everyone laughs with relief.

For security reasons I'm not allowed to help with the cooking, which I'm disappointed about, but despite the many strict rules and regulations, the soldiers are warm and welcoming and, surprisingly, once they begin to relax a little, are actually very good humoured and quite cheeky.

The soldiers explain that a portion of each meal is first fed to the camp dogs, to check if the food has been poisoned. Today, however, is an exception and spoons are handed around the kitchen. The curry is delicious — creamy and spicy, but not too hot. I feel honoured that this has been prepared for me. Cashews are extremely

expensive, with 500 grams costing about 1,000 rupees, or the equivalent of one or two days' salary.

Afterwards, I wander over to the lagoon, but stop when someone shouts at me. The lagoon is off-limits because it is full of land mines. Land mines are a big problem in Sri Lanka and although work is being done to clear them, it is painstakingly slow.

> *'Afterwards, I wander over to the lagoon, but stop when someone shouts at me. The lagoon is off-limits because it is full of land mines.'*

I decide to head over to the cashew nut nursery. It is bigger than I expected, with thousands of small seedlings growing in rows. The cashew seedlings have been donated by Dilmah Conservation as part of a conservation project called Greening Batticaloa. Around 50,000 young cashew plants will be given to local families, to not only assist in rebuilding the environment destroyed by the tsunami but also to provide a much-needed income for the community.

CASHEW NUT CURRY

Serves 4 as a side curry

With emotions still raw from the war, I was a little nervous when I arrived at the 233 Brigade in Vakarai to stay with the Sri Lankan Army. However, like most Sri Lankans, the soldiers were incredibly warm and welcoming and we had a lot of fun cooking this cashew curry in their mess kitchen. It was a unique experience and at times felt quite surreal, but I loved it and would go back in a heartbeat!

INGREDIENTS

500 g (1 lb 2 oz/3¼ cups) raw cashew nuts, soaked in water for 3 hours

1 teaspoon ground turmeric

1½ teaspoons Manike's thuna paha (page 153) (or store-bought roasted curry powder)

1½ teaspoons unroasted chilli powder*

1 teaspoon freshly ground black pepper, plus ½ teaspoon extra

1 teaspoon salt, plus extra to taste

16 cm (6¼ inch) piece rampe (pandanus) leaf*, cut into 4 cm (1½ inch) pieces

1 clove garlic, sliced

1 red onion*, sliced

500 ml (17 fl oz/2 cups) coconut milk*

250 ml (9 fl oz/1 cup) coconut cream*

3 thin green chillies*, cut in half lengthways

1 sprig curry leaves, leaves picked

METHOD

Drain the soaked cashews, then place in a wok or heavy-based saucepan with the turmeric, thuna paha, chilli powder, pepper, salt, rampe, garlic and half the sliced onion. Add the coconut milk and stir to combine. Bring to the boil, then cover, reduce the heat to low and simmer for 20 minutes, stirring occasionally, until the cashews are tender.

Stir in the coconut cream, check for seasoning, then add salt to taste. Add the chillies, curry leaves, the rest of the onion and the extra pepper. Simmer for a further 2 minutes, uncovered, then remove from the heat. Serve with a main curry and rice.

THE NORTH
Jaffna Peninsula

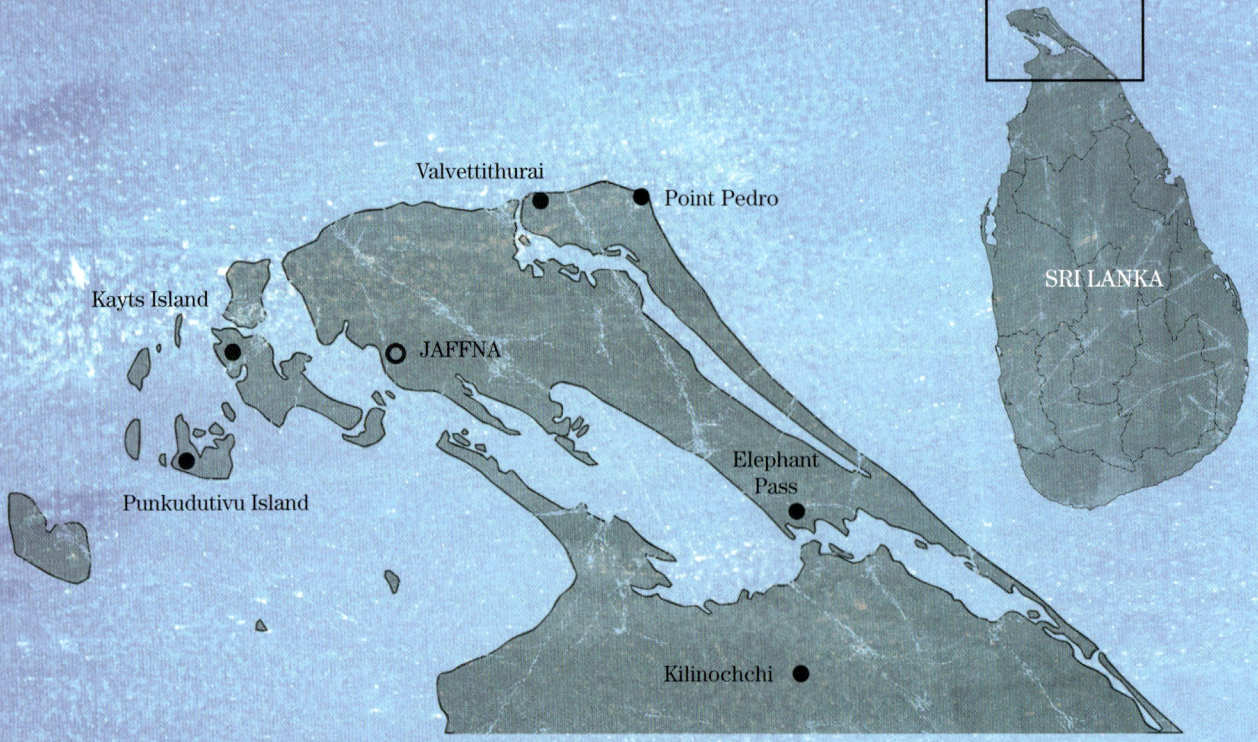

Kayts Island

Valvettithurai

Point Pedro

JAFFNA

Punkudutivu Island

Elephant Pass

Kilinochchi

SRI LANKA

For almost thirty years, the Jaffna Peninsula was cut off from the rest of Sri Lanka and run by the Tamil Tigers (LTTE). When the civil war ended in 2009, the peninsula was re-opened. Although scarred by the conflict and the devastating tsunami in 2004, Jaffna is alluringly beautiful and the people, despite all the hardship they have endured, are surprisingly warm and welcoming.

Jaffna cuisine is the most distinct in Sri Lanka and the people are incredibly proud of it. Renowned for its spicy dishes and use of fresh seafood, Jaffna is especially famous for its crab curry and *odiyal kool*, a spicy seafood soup. The preparation of these dishes is something of a mystery to people from other areas of the island.

With the war over, Jaffna is bouncing back fast. The people possess a unique resilience and determination that is both inspiring and exciting. They exude a positive energy and once you tap into it, it is hard to leave.

COOKING & LIVING
FROM THE HEART
Bamini

When I met Bamini on my first visit to the Jaffna Peninsula earlier in the year, I was humbled by her unshakable resilience. Her jovial demeanour and warm personality downplayed the struggles she has endured. She has survived bomb blasts, shellings, starvation, refugee camps, a tsunami, and lost her husband one month before the civil war ended — most people would have just given up. But this was not an option for Bamini and that is what I love about her. With three young children to support, providing for them and giving them a good education is what matters most to her.

Bamini is from Valvettithurai, a small fishing village on the peninsula's north coast. Famous for being the birthplace of the Tamil Tiger leader, Valvettithurai is, ironically, peaceful and picturesque. If it weren't for the soldiers who occasionally pedal past with rifles slung over their shoulders, I would have thought I was in paradise.

I've been invited to return to Bamini's, to learn how to cook traditional Jaffna cuisine and also some dishes found only in Valvettithurai. Bamini's house is tucked away down a sandy path, a few metres from the beach. When I find my way into her kitchen I know I'm in for a treat. Jars filled with unnamed spices line the shelves; a huge mortar and pestle for pounding spices rests by the wood stove, which houses an array of *thaachchi*, a traditional metal cooking pot similar to a wok.

Bamini is very proud of her cooking, and rightly so. You won't find any cookbooks in her kitchen and when I explain what they are, she looks puzzled and asks, 'Why do you need them?' Like most Sri Lankans, Bamini cooks from her heart, from oral recipes that have been handed down through the generations. She is famous among the locals for her *thosai*, a savoury pancake made from a fermented batter of ground rice and black gram. With no refrigerator, Bamini cooks her food fresh daily, using seasonal ingredients and fresh seafood.

However, it has not always been like this for Bamini and her family; for ten years they survived mostly on food rations. Bamini shows me her last ration card from 2010, and explains the food she missed most during this time was rice.

'There just wasn't enough rice issued. I couldn't make things like string hoppers or *pittu*,' she says. 'I could still buy rice and other food, but it was very expensive. I once paid 5,000 rupees (half her month's salary today) for one packet of powdered milk for the baby. Eventually we ran out of money, so I had to sell all my jewellery, which included family heirlooms given to me by my parents when I married.'

187

While these memories will never leave her, there is no shortage of food in Bamini's house today and a feast is being prepared. Bamini has enlisted the help of her *amma* (mother) and *akka* (older sister) Puwanageetha, and her good friend Jayamathi.

While Bamini's *amma* carefully lays out banana leaves on the floor, she tells me they have prepared one of her all-time favourite dishes, *puli arnam*, a tamarind fish soup. 'When I was pregnant with Bamini, I ate *puli arnam* every day,' she says.

They have also prepared one of Bamini's favourite dishes: fried dried fish with tempered onions, curd chillies and *pittu* (a mixture of steamed rice flour and scraped coconut). 'When she was a child, she mainly liked spicy snacks, not sweets,' her mother says. 'Except once in a while she would ask for *certaikkai*.' *Certaikkai* is a sesame seed sweet famous in Valvettithurai and is not found in other parts of Sri Lanka. I'm excited to learn we are making it this afternoon.

When I sit down cross-legged on the floor (which I later learn doubles as the bedroom and living room), I can hardly wait for the dishes to be spooned onto my banana leaf. In quick succession the women start piling on the food. They remain standing and stare at me while I eat, eagerly waiting for a patch of leaf to reveal itself so they can pile on more food. From their beaming smiles and the constant wobble of their heads, I know I have impressed them with my healthy appetite, tolerance for spicy food and ability to eat with my hand.

Despite the variety of dishes I am sampling, the flavours meld surprisingly well in my mouth — a perfect combination of spicy, salty, sweet and sour. The dish that intrigues me most is the fried dried fish. On its own it is pungent and extremely salty, but when paired with the sweet tempered onions, soft *pittu* and spicy curd chillies it is quite unlike anything I have ever eaten and leaves me hungry for more.

As I eat, Bamini tells me about her dried fish business. She explains how she used to work for a dried fish vendor, but now works for herself. She buys fresh fish from the local fishermen, which she washes, salts and dries in the sun and then sells directly to the wholesalers. She puts her arm around her friend and says, 'We both make more money this way.'

Bamini and Jayamathi were fortunate enough to be given equipment, such as scales, knives, baskets, netting and salt, from the MJF Charitable Foundation so they could start processing their own dried fish. 'The tools they gave us meant we could be independent over our livelihoods.'

'On its own it is pungent and extremely salty, but when paired with the sweet tempered onions, soft pittu *and spicy curd chillies it is quite unlike anything I have ever eaten and leaves me hungry for more.'*

The Foundation has helped more than 200 women on the Jaffna Peninsula who were widowed by the war, by providing them with the necessary tools to establish their own businesses, as well as providing counselling to help them deal with the psychological wounds from the war.

Bamini and Jayamathi are keen to find ways to increase their earning capacity, and next week they plan to buy extra fish from the proceeds they make selling Bamini's *thosai* at the upcoming Hindu festival. Unable to turn down the chance to witness a Hindu festival and the opportunity to learn Bamini's famous *thosai* recipe, I decide to stay a few more days.

BAMINI'S ROASTED CURRY POWDER

Makes 5 tablespoons

If you make only one recipe from Bamini's selection, make sure it is this one. It will change the flavour of any curry you make and it's what gives her recipes such a distinctive taste. Bamini's curry powder is now a staple in my kitchen, and I can't imagine cooking a curry without it. You need to start this recipe a day before you need it, to allow time for drying the spices in the sun.

INGREDIENTS

2 sprigs curry leaves, leaves picked

2 teaspoons fennel seeds

2 tablespoons coriander seeds

1 teaspoon black peppercorns

1 tablespoon red rice*

8 dried long red chillies*

3 cloves garlic, thinly sliced

1 cinnamon stick, broken in half

METHOD

Wash the curry leaves, fennel seeds, coriander seeds, peppercorns and red rice separately, then place them on separate plates and leave to dry in the sun for a day.

Dry-roast the sun-dried and the remaining ingredients separately in a small wok or heavy-based frying pan over low heat for 1–2 minutes, or until fragrant, shaking the pan continuously. Remove from the heat and transfer to a small bowl to cool.

Put all the cooled ingredients into a mortar and pestle (or spice grinder) and pound into a fine powder. Store in an airtight container for up to 2 months.

DUBBI NANDU

Serves 4 as a snack

Bamini made this dish as a snack while we were preparing the odiyal kool. *She marinated the flesh of the* dubbi nandu *(balmain bugs) in a blend of spices and then fried them, finishing with a squeeze of lime juice. Once I tasted them, I knew I would be making this at home.*

INGREDIENTS

800 g (1 lb 12 oz/about 4) green (raw) balmain or moreton bay bugs (or cooked)

3 teaspoons Bamini's roasted curry powder (page 195) (or store-bought roasted curry powder)

1½ teaspoons salt

200 g (7 oz/about 15) small pink Asian shallots*, peeled and left whole

500 ml (17 fl oz/2 cups) vegetable oil, for frying

1 red onion*, halved and thinly sliced

3–4 thin green chillies*, halved lengthways

1 lime, cut into wedges

METHOD

Bring a large saucepan of water to the boil. Add the balmain bugs and boil for 5 minutes, or until just cooked. Drain and rinse under cold running water or plunge into iced water to stop the cooking process. If using cooked bugs, you can skip this step.

To remove the meat, take the tail in one hand and the head in the other, and twist hard so the tail and head separate. Discard the head. Using a pair of kitchen scissors, cut down the edges of the underside to peel back the shell; you can then easily remove the flesh from the tail. Devein and place in a bowl, discarding the shell. Add the curry powder, salt and shallots and mix well. Extract the shallots and set them aside.

Heat the oil in a small wok or saucepan over medium heat and fry the shallots for 3 minutes, or until golden brown. Remove with a slotted spoon and place in a bowl. Fry the marinated pieces of balmain bug for 1–2 minutes, or until golden brown. Remove with a slotted spoon and add to the fried shallots. Then fry the onion for 4 minutes, or until golden brown, and add to the other fried ingredients. Finally, fry the chillies for 2 minutes. Mix all the fried ingredients together and transfer to a serving plate. Serve warm with lime wedges.

FRIED DRIED FISH

Serves 4 as a side dish

When Bamini made me this traditional dish from Valvettithurai I was a bit apprehensive — dried fish has quite a pungent odour — but to my surprise it was very tasty. If you can't find good-quality dried fish, fresh fish is a wonderful alternative, but you will need to double the quantity of salt and roasted curry powder.

INGREDIENTS

200 g (7 oz/about 15) small pink Asian
  shallots*, peeled and halved
140 g (5 oz) dried fish*, cut into 2–3 cm
  (¾–1¼ inch) pieces (or 500 g/ 1 lb 2 oz)
  white-fleshed fish such as baby
  barramundi, cut into cutlets about
  1.5 cm (⅝ inch) thick)

2 teaspoons salt
2 teaspoons Bamini's roasted curry
  powder (page 195) (or store-bought
  roasted curry powder)
vegetable oil, for deep-frying
20 g (¾ oz/1 cup) curd chillies (page 202)
  (or store-bought)

METHOD

Place the shallots and dried fish in two separate bowls. Combine the salt and curry powder, then sprinkle half over the shallots and half over the dried fish. Mix well and set aside.

Fill a small wok or heavy-based saucepan one-third full of oil and heat to approximately 150°C (300°F) (a cube of bread dropped into the oil will brown in 35 seconds). Deep-fry the curd chillies for 30–60 seconds, or until dark brown and crisp, then remove with a slotted spoon and drain on paper towel. Deep-fry the shallots for 2–3 minutes, or until golden brown, then remove and drain on paper towel. Deep-fry the dried fish pieces for 2 minutes (3 minutes if using fresh fish), or until dark brown and crisp. Remove with a slotted spoon and drain on paper towel.

Transfer the fish to a serving plate, and put the fried shallots and curd chillies into small bowls. Serve with pittu (page 218).

CURD CHILLIES
Makes 40 g (1½ oz/2 cups)

When Bamini and Jayamathi offered me fried whole chillies, I thought they were playing a joke, so I cautiously nibbled at one. Much to my surprise, my mouth didn't catch on fire and they were really good — crunchy, salty and smoky. Curd chillies are a great accompaniment to any curry and are easy to make, but they take a week to dry in the sun. Pre-dried ones are available from Sri Lankan specialty stores, and these just need to be deep-fried before serving.

INGREDIENTS

250 g (9 oz) medium green chillies*
  (see note)

125 g (4½ oz/½ cup) curd* (or thick,
  natural yoghurt)

3 teaspoons salt, dissolved in
  3 teaspoons warm water

METHOD

Cut off the stalks from the chillies and then make two 5 mm (¼ inch) slits in the middle of each chilli. If they aren't pierced, the chillies can explode when you deep-fry them. Place the slit chillies in a bowl and add the curd and salty water; mix well, making sure all the chillies are evenly coated in curd. Remove the chillies and place on a terracotta plate and leave in the sun, uncovered, for a week to dry out, bringing them inside at night.

Once the chillies have absorbed all the curd and dried out, store in an airtight container. When needed, deep-fry in batches in hot vegetable oil for 30–60 seconds, or until dark brown and crisp. Remove with a slotted spoon and drain on paper towel. Serve as an accompaniment to curries or eat as a spicy snack.

NOTE: As chillies vary in heat, ask your Sri Lankan grocer to recommend the best type of chilli to use for this recipe. You want a chilli that is not too hot or large.

Hidden Kitchens of Sri Lanka

PULI ARNAM

Serves 4

This light tamarind fish soup is superb — mild in flavour, with a slight tanginess and fiery kick. This is Bamini's mother's favourite dish and it's also my mum's favourite from the recipes I brought back from Sri Lanka. It's easy to make and delicious eaten on its own.

INGREDIENTS

4–6 dried long red chillies*, stalks removed

300 g (10½ oz/about 20) small pink Asian shallots*, peeled and left whole

160 g (5¾ oz) tamarind pulp*, soaked in 750 ml (26 fl oz/3 cups) warm water

1 kg (2 lb 4 oz) whole white-fleshed fish (such as snapper), cut into 4 cm (1½ inch) thick cutlets (see note)

2 teaspoons salt

METHOD

Bring a saucepan of water to the boil. Add the dried chillies and shallots and boil for about 20 minutes, or until soft. Meanwhile, prepare the tamarind pulp following the method on page 261. Set the tamarind water aside.

Strain the cooked shallots and chillies and then place them in a food processor and process into a paste.

In a large heavy-based saucepan, combine the shallot paste, the fish pieces (including the head and tail), salt, tamarind water and 500 ml (17 fl oz/2 cups) water (there should be enough liquid to cover the fish; if not, add a little extra water). Bring to the boil, then cover, reduce the heat to low and simmer gently for 10 minutes, or until the fish is just cooked. Serve with rice.

NOTE: Traditionally, this dish is made with a whole fish, cut through the bone into thick cutlets. You can ask your fishmonger to cut the cutlets for you, but don't forget to ask for the head and tail, as these are added to the soup for flavour. However, if you prefer to eat fish without the bones, use 600 g (1 lb 5 oz) thick white fish fillets (skin on), such as blue eye cod.

ODIYAL KOOL

Serves 6–8

This thick seafood soup is one of Jaffna's signature dishes and each family makes it slightly differently. The soup is thickened with odiyal flour, which is made from the roots of a young palmyra plant. For many Sri Lankan families kool is not just about the food, it's about bringing family and friends together and should always be prepared and eaten by a lot of people.

INGREDIENTS

6 dried long red chillies*, stalks removed

1½ teaspoons black peppercorns

80 g (2¾ oz/2 tablespoons) tamarind
    pulp*, soaked in 250 ml (9 fl oz/1 cup)
    warm water

100 g (3½ oz/⅔ cup) odiyal flour*

1 small whole bulb garlic

salt

80 g (2¾ oz/3 tablespoons) red
    samba rice*

300 g (10½ oz) pumpkin, peeled and
    cut into 2 cm (¾ inch) cubes

350 g (12 oz) manioc* (cassava)
    (or 300 g/10½ oz frozen), peeled
    and cut into 2 cm (¾ inch) cubes

100 g (3½ oz) bitter gourd* (bitter
    melon), seeds removed and cut into
    1 cm (½ inch) pieces

16 green (raw) king prawns, peeled and
    deveined, leaving heads and tails intact

2 small blue swimmer crabs
    (about 330 g/11½ oz each), washed
    and quartered, guts removed

200 g (7 oz) firm white fish fillets
    (such as whiting), cut into 4 cm
    (1½ inch) pieces

200 g (7 oz) cuttlefish, cut into
    4 cm (1½ inch) pieces

150 g (5½ oz) snake beans*, cut into 3 cm
    (1¼ inch) pieces

15 g (½ oz/½ cup) drumstick leaves*
    (or English spinach leaves, chopped)

100 g (3½ oz) dried fish*, burnt over
    a flame, then chopped into 2 cm (¾ inch)
    pieces (optional)

METHOD

To make the chilli paste, soak the dried chillies in water for 1 hour until soft. Drain and place the chillies in a small food processor with the peppercorns and 2 tablespoons water. Process to a smooth paste.

Prepare the tamarind pulp following the method on page 261. Set the tamarind water aside. Mix the odiyal flour with 250 ml (9 fl oz/1 cup) water in a small bowl and leave to soak for 30 minutes, or until it forms a thick paste.

Peel the garlic cloves. Using a mortar and pestle, pound the garlic and 2 teaspoons salt into a paste. Set aside.

Wash the samba rice well, and place in a large stockpot with 1.25 litres (44 fl oz/5 cups) water. Bring to the boil, then reduce the heat, cover and simmer for 25 minutes. Add the pumpkin, manioc, bitter gourd and 1 teaspoon salt; simmer with the lid on for a further 5 minutes, or until the vegetables and rice are tender. Add the prawns, crab pieces, fish, cuttlefish, snake beans, drumstick leaves and enough water to cover (about 500 ml/17 fl oz/2 cups). Bring to the boil, then reduce the heat, cover and simmer for 5 minutes.

Add the chilli paste, garlic paste and burnt dried fish (if using) to the pot. Gently stir to combine and simmer for a further 2 minutes. Add the odiyal flour paste, gently stir to combine, then add the tamarind water. Simmer for 2 minutes, or until the kool is thick and glossy. Season to taste with salt, remove the pot from the heat and serve.

CRAB CURRY

Serves 4

Jaffna is renowned for its abundant seafood and a visit to the region isn't complete without tasting their famous crab curry. We cooked the curry over an open fire in Bamini's garden and the flavours were incredible! Be prepared to get a bit messy when eating this dish, but I can assure you it is worth it.

INGREDIENTS

4 blue swimmer crabs (about 400 g/14 oz each) (or 2 live mud crabs, about 800 g (1 lb 12 oz) each)

4 cloves garlic, thinly sliced

2 cm (¾ inch) piece ginger, thinly sliced

1 teaspoon salt, plus extra to taste

1 tablespoon vegetable oil

1 red onion*, thinly sliced

1–2 thin green chillies*, halved lengthways (optional)

3 vine-ripened tomatoes, diced

1 teaspoon fennel seeds

1 teaspoon fenugreek seeds

2 teaspoons dried chilli pieces*

1 teaspoon unroasted chilli powder*

375 ml (13 fl oz/1½ cups) coconut milk*

3 sprigs curry leaves, leaves picked

juice of ½ lime

METHOD

If using live mud crabs, place them in the freezer for 1–2 hours until they are completely immobilised before you begin chopping them.

Remove the triangular flap under the crab and discard it, then lift off and remove the head, keeping the head to cook with the rest of the crab for presentation. Remove the gills and any yellow 'mustard'. Wash the crabs. Cut in half, then pull off the big claws. Using the back of a large knife, tap the claws to crack them; this allows the flavours to seep in while cooking. Wash the crab pieces and set aside.

Using a mortar and pestle, pound the garlic, ginger and salt into a paste. Heat the oil in a large wok or heavy-based saucepan and cook the onion over medium heat for 3 minutes. Add the chillies and the garlic and ginger paste and cook for 1 minute. Stir in the tomatoes, fennel seeds, fenugreek seeds, dried chilli pieces and chilli powder; cook for 1 minute. Add the coconut milk, curry leaves and crab pieces; simmer for a further 10 minutes, or until the sauce has thickened and almost completely reduced, making sure to turn the crab regularly. Remove from the heat, add the lime juice and season to taste with salt.

211

IDLI
Makes 20

These fluffy, steamed savoury cakes, traditionally made from a fermented batter of black gram and rice flour, are perfect for mopping up curry sauces. Bamini uses semolina instead of rice flour, which makes hers extra soft. You'll need to start this recipe at least one day before you want to serve it and you will need an idli steamer, which are available from Sri Lankan and Indian specialty stores. Bamini generously gave me her steamer as a parting gift.

INGREDIENTS

55 g (2 oz/¼ cup) whole black gram*
   (ulundu) (or store-bought skinned
   black gram)
285 g (10 oz/1½ cups) coarse semolina

1 teaspoon bicarbonate of soda
¼ teaspoon salt
vegetable oil, for cooking

METHOD

Soak the black gram in 250 ml (9 fl oz/1 cup) water for 8 hours (skinned black gram also needs to be soaked). Wash and drain. If using whole black gram, remove the outer skins by vigorously rubbing and squeezing them between your fingers and palms. Continue until most of the skins are removed (this will take about 1 hour). Discard the skins, retaining only the white bit of the black gram. Place the skinned black gram in a food processor with 185 ml (6 fl oz/¾ cup) water and process to form a thick but fine paste. Leave the paste in the processor.

Line a bamboo steamer with two layers of muslin or a piece of non-stick baking paper. Place the semolina in the steamer and cover with the lid. Fill a wok about one-third full with water and bring to the boil. Place the steamer in the wok, ensuring the bottom of the steamer isn't touching the water, then reduce to a simmer and steam the semolina for 4 minutes.

Add the semolina and about 185 ml (6 fl oz/¾ cup) water to the gram paste, and process to combine (the consistency should be thick but runny). Transfer to a large bowl, cover with plastic wrap and a tea towel and leave to ferment in a warm place for 8 hours or overnight.

When fermented, dissolve the bicarbonate of soda in 1 tablespoon water and add to the semolina mixture along with the salt. Mix well. If needed, gradually add a little water (about 2 tablespoons). The consistency should be thick but still runny.

To cook the idli, lightly brush the idli moulds with oil, then spoon in the mixture, cover and steam for 10–15 minutes. To test if the idli are cooked, remove one with a spoon, hold it in the palm of your hand and with your other hand tap it lightly; if the idli bounces, it is ready. Remove the remaining idli from the moulds with a spoon. Serve hot with sambar (page 217) and green coconut chutney (page 213).

GREEN COCONUT CHUTNEY

Makes about 600 g (1 lb 5 oz/2½ cups)

When Bamini was making this chutney I knew instantly I was going to like it because I'm a big fan of fresh coconut. As soon as the chutney was finished, I ate it by the spoonful, straight from the bowl.

INGREDIENTS

30 g (1 oz/¾ tablespoon) tamarind pulp*, soaked in 60 ml (2 fl oz/¼ cup) warm water

vegetable oil, for deep-frying

60 g (2¼ oz) long green chillies*, halved lengthways

pinch of cumin seeds

330 g (11½ oz/2¾ cups) freshly scraped coconut*

1 teaspoon salt

FOR TEMPERING

60 ml (2 fl oz/¼ cup) vegetable oil

1 teaspoon black mustard seeds

½ red onion*, thinly sliced

2 teaspoons cumin seeds

½ teaspoon fenugreek seeds

1 sprig curry leaves, leaves picked

2 dried long red chillies*, stalks removed, chopped

METHOD

Prepare the tamarind pulp following the method on page 261. Set the tamarind water aside.

Fill a small wok or saucepan one-third full of oil and heat to approximately 150°C (300°F) (a cube of bread dropped into the oil will brown in 35 seconds). Deep-fry the chillies for 1 minute, or until the skins start to blister and turn slightly white (they won't be crispy). Remove with a slotted spoon.

Put the fried chillies in a food processor with the cumin seeds, 120 g (4¼ oz/1 cup) of the coconut and 60 ml (2 fl oz/¼ cup) water; process into a fine paste. Transfer to a bowl. Process the remaining coconut with 125 ml (4 fl oz/½ cup) water into a thick paste, then add the chilli and coconut paste and process again. Add the tamarind water and salt; process, adding a little more water if needed (the consistency should be light and a little runny). Transfer to a bowl and set aside.

For tempering, heat the oil in a small wok or frying pan over medium heat and add the mustard seeds. When the seeds start to pop, add the onion and cook for 2 minutes, or until the onion is tender but not brown. Add the cumin seeds, fenugreek seeds, curry leaves and dried chillies and cook for 2–4 minutes, stirring constantly, until the onions are dark golden. Remove from the heat and strain through a sieve. Add half of the tempered onion mixture to the chilli coconut paste; stir to combine. Transfer to a bowl and garnish with the remaining tempered onion mixture. Serve with idli (page 212) or thosai (page 228).

SAMBAR

Serves 6–8

A spicy lentil and vegetable stew, served with idli *for breakfast or lunch.*

INGREDIENTS

80 g (2¾ oz/2 tablespoons) tamarind
  pulp*, soaked in 125 ml (4 fl oz/½ cup)
  warm water

300 g (10½ oz) pumpkin, peeled, cut
  into 3 cm (1¼ inch) cubes

300 g (10½ oz) long, thin light purple
  eggplants, cut into 3 cm (1¼ inch)
  pieces

200 g (7 oz) snake beans*, cut into 4 cm
  (1½ inch) pieces

300 g (10½ oz) potatoes, peeled, cut into
  3 cm (1¼ inch) cubes

350 g (12 oz) manioc* (cassava)
  (or 300 g/10½ oz frozen), peeled,
  cut into 3 cm (1¼ inch) cubes

190 g (6¾ oz/1 cup) red lentils, washed well

1½ teaspoons Bamini's roasted curry
  powder (page 195) (or store-bought
  roasted curry powder)

2 teaspoons unroasted chilli powder*

2 teaspoons ground turmeric

2 teaspoons salt

250 ml (9 fl oz/1 cup) coconut cream*

FOR TEMPERING

125 ml (4 fl oz/½ cup) vegetable oil

1 tablespoon black mustard seeds

2 red onions*, thinly sliced

1 tablespoon cumin seeds

1 teaspoon fenugreek seeds

3 sprigs curry leaves, leaves picked

3–4 dried long red chillies*, chopped

METHOD

Prepare the tamarind pulp following the method on page 261. Set the tamarind water aside.

Place all the vegetables and the red lentils into a stockpot, then add 1.5 litres (52 fl oz/6 cups) water, or enough to cover. Bring to the boil, then cover, reduce the heat to low and simmer for 10 minutes, or until the vegetables are almost cooked and the lentils are soft (the lentils will absorb most of the liquid). Add the curry powder, chilli powder, turmeric and salt; simmer, uncovered, for 5 minutes. Add the coconut cream and tamarind water and bring to just below the boil, stirring regularly so the coconut cream doesn't split. Add a little more water if needed (the consistency should be liquidy). Remove from the heat just before it boils and set aside.

For tempering, heat the oil in a small wok or frying pan over medium heat and add the mustard seeds. When the seeds start to pop, add the onions and cook for 5 minutes, stirring regularly, until the onions are tender but not brown. Add the cumin seeds, fenugreek seeds, curry leaves and dried chillies and cook for 3–4 minutes, stirring constantly, until the onions are dark golden. Remove from the heat and strain through a sieve. Add the tempered onion mixture to the sambar (reserving a spoonful for garnish) and stir to combine. Season to taste with salt, and garnish with the reserved tempered onion mixture. Serve with steamed rice or idli (page 212) and green coconut chutney (page 213).

PITTU

Serves 4–6

Pittu *is a mixture of steamed rice flour and fresh coconut, and it's a great alternative to rice. Knowing it was one of my favourites, Bamini cooked it often, usually serving it with curry or fried dried fish, and for breakfast with jackfruit.* **Pittu** *is commonly steamed in a cylinder-shaped mould, but Bamini steams hers the Jaffna way, in a cone-shaped palmyra basket that sits inside a tall narrow pot.*

INGREDIENTS

140 g (5 oz/1 cup) roasted red rice flour*

140 g (5 oz/1 cup) roasted white rice flour*

pinch of salt

250 ml (9 fl oz/1 cup) boiling water

240 g (8½ oz/2 cups) freshly scraped coconut*, plus 2 tablespoons extra for steaming

METHOD

Combine the red and white rice flours in a large bowl with a pinch of salt. Gradually sprinkle the boiling water, a little at a time, onto the flour, stirring continuously with a wooden spoon until it resembles small breadcrumbs. To test if you have added enough water, squeeze a small amount of mixture in your hand — it should stay together without breaking.

Transfer the mixture to a large shallow dish or bowl. Add the coconut and mix with your fingers. Then, use the side of a large metal spoon to break up any lumps that have formed.

Take a woven palmyra basket and fill the bottom with 1 tablespoon of the extra coconut, then spoon on half the rice flour and coconut mixture, making sure you don't press the mixture down or it will stick together. Place the basket into the pittu steamer, then cover and steam for 5–10 minutes. To check if the mixture is cooked, tap the top lightly with your fingertips; if it bounces back it's ready. Remove from the steamer and turn out onto a plate. Repeat with the remaining mixture.

NOTE: Palmyra baskets and pittu steamers are available from Sri Lankan specialty stores. Alternatively you could use a fine conical-shaped sieve lined with muslin, placed inside a large deep saucepan; just be careful the bottom of the sieve does not come in contact with the water.

CERTAIKKAI

Serves 4–6 as a snack

This is a traditional fried sesame seed sweet found only in Valvettithurai and not in other parts of Sri Lanka. When we cooked these, neither Bamini nor I could wait for the sweets to cool properly before popping a few in our mouths — they are delicious and very addictive!

INGREDIENTS

¾ tablespoon green gram*
  (dried mung beans)

120 g (4¼ oz/1 cup) fine white rice flour

1½ tablespoons roasted black gram
  (ulundu) flour*

100 g (3½ oz/⅔ cup) white sesame seeds

125 ml (4 fl oz/½ cup) coconut cream*

80 ml (2½ fl oz/⅓ cup) coconut milk*

500 ml (17 fl oz/2 cups) vegetable oil,
  for frying

440 g (15½ oz/2 cups) sugar

METHOD

To prepare the mixed gram flour, dry-roast the green gram in a heavy-based frying pan over medium heat for 4 minutes. Cool slightly, then using a mortar and pestle (or spice grinder), pound the green gram into a fine powder. Transfer to a bowl and combine with the rice flour and black gram flour.

Sift the mixed gram flour into a large bowl and mix in the sesame seeds. Put the coconut cream and coconut milk in a small saucepan over medium heat and bring to just below the boil. Remove from the heat and pour over the flour and sesame mixture. Using a wooden spoon, stir until the mixture starts to come together, then use your hands to knead into a pliable dough.

Take ½ tablespoon of the dough into your hand and squeeze it a few times so the oil starts to release from the sesame seeds. Shape into a small log about 8 cm (3¼ inch) long and 1 cm (½ inch) thick. Tear off a little piece of dough and roll it into a small ball, the size of a hazelnut, making sure all edges are smooth and there are no cracks. Repeat with the remaining dough.

Heat the oil in a wok to approximately 150°C (300°F) (a cube of bread dropped into the oil will brown in 35 seconds). Working in two batches, fry the dough balls for 4–5 minutes, tossing them regularly in the hot oil until golden brown. Remove with a slotted spoon, drain on paper towel, then set aside to cool in a large deep bowl.

To make the syrup, bring 250 ml (9 fl oz/1 cup) water to the boil in a small saucepan, add the sugar, then reduce the heat to low and simmer for 20 minutes, or until the mixture has reduced by half. Remove from the heat and while hot, slowly pour the syrup over the sesame balls, a little at a time. Using a wooden spoon, mix well, making sure all the balls are evenly coated in the syrup. It's important that you keep stirring until the syrup sets or the balls will clump together. Allow to cool before serving.

RASAVALLI PUDDING

Serves 6

This dessert is a regional specialty made from a purple yam called rasavalli, which grows on the Jaffna Peninsula. When Bamini made this I was a bit sceptical because of its unusual violet colour, but the flavours were surprisingly delicate and it tasted divine. Bamini obviously thought so too, as I caught her licking the wooden spoon!

INGREDIENTS

550 g (1 lb 4 oz) rasavalli* (or use 500 g
 (1 lb 2 oz) frozen rasavalli), peeled
 and cut into 1.5 cm (⅝ inch) cubes

50 g (1¾ oz/¼ cup) sago

110 g (3¾ oz/½ cup) sugar

250 ml (9 fl oz/1 cup) coconut cream*

250 ml (9 fl oz/1 cup) coconut milk*

1 teaspoon roasted black gram
 (ulundu) flour*

METHOD

Place the rasavalli cubes in a large saucepan, add just enough water to cover, then bring to the boil. Reduce the heat and simmer for 10–12 minutes, or until the rasavalli is soft. Remove from the heat and use the back of a spoon to roughly mash the rasavalli.

Return the pan to a low heat and slowly stir in the sago. When the sago is mixed in, stir in the sugar, then gradually add the coconut cream and coconut milk. Bring to the boil, then reduce the heat to medium and cook for 10–12 minutes, or until the sago is cooked and turns transparent (stir regularly so the coconut milk doesn't split and the mixture doesn't catch on the bottom of the pan). Sprinkle on the black gram flour and stir well. Remove from the heat and serve hot.

A TEMPLE FEAST
Valvettithurai
Hindu Festival

The streets of Valvettithurai are a hive of activity and a blur of bright colours. You can feel the excitement brewing in the air. Today marks the beginning of a fifteen-day Hindu festival, held in honour of Lord Shiva's wife, goddess Amman, the patron goddess of Valvettithurai's main *kovil* (temple). The festival is for devotees to give thanks to the gods for all the good things bestowed upon them during the year.

Pre-festival activities have set the momentum for things to come: streets have been washed with water, portable lamps erected, and shopfronts decorated with palmyra palms and bunches of bananas. Women in bright silk saris collect jasmine flowers to wear in their hair, while the men make the final touches to the colourful banners and flags that decorate the chariots. Specific ceremonies are set to take place each day throughout the festival, and today is the hoisting of the flag ceremony.

My attention is drawn to a stream of smoke coming from a shed behind the *kovil*, and a distinct aroma of curry leaves and mustard seeds frying in oil. I have heard whispers that the *kovil* provides a delicious vegetarian lunch for devotees and visitors each day during the festival and that it is considered a blessing to eat there during this time. I head over to the kitchen and step inside.

Half a dozen massive cooking pots simmering with delicious-looking curries are lined up against the wall, and an elderly man is hunched over three large woks on an open fire. In one, he is tempering mustard seeds and curry leaves, to which he adds shredded cabbage and a sprinkling of turmeric. Effortlessly he turns his attention to the other two woks, glistening with hot oil, and plunges pieces of pappadums into one and curd chillies into the other.

I am drawn outside by the sound of music and chanting; the temple grounds have erupted in a flurry of colourful saris, drums, trumpets and flags. The *kovil* priest (*kurrukal*) chants from an ancient text, while another *kurrukal* drapes fine cloth over a statue of goddess Amman, who sits on top of one of the chariots. A flammable torch is doused in coconut oil and then lit, and the parade begins, the musicians leading the way, while others follow behind, pulling the chariots. Every couple of metres the chariots come to a halt and the chanting commences again.

By the time the chariots have completed a full circle around the *kovil*, people start to break away and make their way towards the dining hall. Unsure as to the

correct etiquette, I hold back, but as people start clambering in, I quickly follow. Everyone sits cross-legged on the floor in neat rows: the women on one side and the men on the other. A young boy scurries down the aisles flinging banana leaves at our laps, while another trails behind dragging a massive basket of rice. Men with buckets of food dart up and down the aisles dishing out curries and accompaniments, piling food on my banana leaf until I signal for them to stop. I am a little self-conscious about eating with my hands in front of such a large audience, but soon realise no one even notices I am here.

While the food is delicious, this is not a relaxed dining experience. It is more of a feeding frenzy, and in less than five minutes a new crowd of hungry devotees scurries in. I can't keep up and my dining neighbours change three times before I fold my banana leaf in half to signal that I have finished. It is quickly whisked away and replaced with a small cup of mango *payasam* (sago). I sip slowly, savouring the soothing flavours, as devotees begin clearing up and sweeping the floor around me.

Outside, the chariots have commenced their parade through the streets, so I rush outside to join them. We move slowly along the streets to the pulsating rhythm of drums beating, trumpets blaring and people chanting. When we reach the other side of town, I leave the procession and head over to Bamini's. She has promised to teach me how to make *thosai*, which she and Jayamathi are selling at the festival tonight. They are busy setting up chairs and tables on the road outside Bamini's parents' home.

'You're just in time!' they say, smiling warmly. I help with the preparations, but I'm instructed to leave the container of eggplant curry hidden until it is time to start cooking the *thosai*.

We place the curry on the table — this signals that Bamini is ready to start trading. Then, in no time at all, people flock to the stall; the gas burners can hardly keep up with the demand. Without breaking a sweat, Bamini rhythmically swirls ladles of batter onto the hot *tavas* (cast-iron *roti* pans); when the *thosai* begin to bubble and brown around the edges, she skilfully flips them over. As always, Jayamathi is by her side, chatting and laughing as she spoons eggplant curry onto plates piled high with *thosai*, adding a generous dollop of green coconut chutney and a sprinkle of Bamini's *thosai podi*.

I feel my appetite return and when Jayamathi hands me a plate of *thosai*, everyone huddles around me, eagerly awaiting my reaction. I tear off a piece of the soft pancake and use it to scoop up the juicy pieces of spiced eggplant. I have eaten many *thosai* in Sri Lanka, but this is the best I've ever had. The flavours are incredible: the richness of the fried eggplant and the kick from the *podi* complement the cool coconut chutney and the slightly tangy moist pancake.

Bamini tells me the secret to her *thosai* is to not take any short cuts. She spends days making her batter the traditional way: she first soaks the black gram with fenugreek seeds before she painstakingly peels off the skins, then grinds the gram into a paste before leaving the batter to ferment overnight.

When Bamini hands me another helping, I wonder how I am ever going to leave this place. The food I have eaten and the friendships I have made in Valvettithurai have had a profound effect on me and I vow to return.

THOSAI

Makes 18 (serves 6)

Thosai *are thin pancakes made from a fermented batter of rice and black gram. Bamini uses whole black gram, which she insists is the only way to make* thosai, *but it takes considerable time and patience to peel their skins. To save time, you can use skinned black gram instead — but don't tell Bamini!* Thosai *are cooked on a flat cast-iron pan known as a* tava, *which are available from Sri Lankan and Indian specialty stores. This recipe is a labour of love and it takes a day or two to prepare, but I promise you the results are worth the effort.*

INGREDIENTS

125 g (4½ oz) whole black gram*
   (ulundu) (or store-bought skinned
   black gram)

1 teaspoon fenugreek seeds

125 g (4½ oz) white samba rice*

100 g (3½ oz) red rice*

300 g (10½ oz/2 cups) plain flour

1 teaspoon bicarbonate of soda

½ teaspoon salt

vegetable oil, for cooking

METHOD

Soak the black gram and fenugreek seeds together in plenty of water for 8 hours or overnight (skinned black gram also needs to be soaked). Soak the samba rice and red rice separately for 8 hours.

Wash the black gram well and drain. If using whole black gram, remove the outer skins by vigorously rubbing and squeezing them between your fingers and palms. Continue until most of the skins are removed (this will take about 1 hour). Discard the skins, retaining only the white bit of the black gram. If the skins don't come off easily, the black gram may need to soak for a little longer.

Process the skinned black gram and the fenugreek seeds in a small food processor, gradually adding small amounts of water to make a smooth, thick creamy paste. Transfer to a large bowl and set aside. Process the samba rice, gradually adding small amounts of water to make a smooth, thick sticky paste. Transfer to the bowl with the black gram paste. Repeat this process with the red rice, making sure the paste is very smooth (but not runny), otherwise the thosai won't have the right texture when you cook them. Add to the bowl with the other pastes and stir to combine (the bowl needs to be double the size of the combined paste mixture, as the batter will increase in volume when fermented).

Sift in the flour and bicarbonate of soda, mixing well with a whisk or wooden spoon, while gradually adding enough water to form a smooth, thick paste. Cover with plastic wrap and a tea towel, and leave in a warm place for 8 hours to ferment. If the temperature is cool, you may need to turn the oven on, to warm up the kitchen a little.

Once the mixture has fermented, add the salt. Gradually mix in small amounts of water to make a pancake-like batter. The consistency of the mixture should be thick and flowing, but not so thin that it's runny. If the texture is not right, add a little extra flour or more water.

Heat a tava or large cast-iron pan over medium heat and brush lightly with oil. When the tava is hot, quickly pour in a ladleful (about 80 ml/2½ fl oz/⅓ cup) of batter in the shape of a spiral, then using the base of the ladle, quickly smooth the batter, spreading it outwards to create a thin circular pancake (16–18 cm (6¼–7 inches) in diameter). Cook for 1–2 minutes, or until little bubbles start to form and the top of the thosai is almost cooked (it should look like a large, thin crumpet). Using a wide spatula, carefully flip it over and cook for another 1 minute, or until golden brown. As you finish each thosai, transfer it to a plate (stack the thosai on top of each other) and keep warm while you cook the rest, making sure to smear the tava with oil before you cook each one.

To serve, place two thosai on each plate and add a couple of tablespoons of fried eggplant curry (page 233) in the centre. Top with a spoonful of green coconut chutney (page 213) and a generous sprinkle of thosai podi (page 232).

THOSAI PODI

Makes 280 g (10 oz/2⅓ cups)

This dry-roasted ground spice mix is sprinkled on top of thosai *and sometimes* idli. *This recipe was given to Bamini by her* amma. *It is one of the best things I have ever tasted and Bamini's* thosai *would not be complete without it. Although it's not traditional, I also like to sprinkle it on top of curries.*

INGREDIENTS

320 g (11¼ oz/2⅔ cups) freshly
   scraped coconut*

50 g (1¾ oz/¼ cup) red rice*

55 g (2 oz/¼ cup) whole black
   gram* (ulundu)

15 dried long red chillies*, stalks removed
   and roughly chopped

1 tablespoon fennel seeds

3 teaspoons black peppercorns

1½ teaspoons salt

METHOD

Heat a wok or large heavy-based frying pan over medium heat and dry-roast the coconut for 7–8 minutes, stirring continuously, until the coconut is a dark golden brown. Set aside to cool. Dry-roast the red rice and black gram separately for 4 minutes each, and set aside to cool.

   Using a mortar and pestle (or spice grinder), pound the red rice into a powder, then transfer to a large bowl. Pound the black gram into a coarse flour, then place in the bowl with the rice powder. Pound the dried chillies, fennel seeds, peppercorns and salt into a rough powder, similar in texture to chilli flakes, then place in the bowl. Add the roasted coconut and stir to combine. Store in an airtight container for 2–4 weeks.

FRIED EGGPLANT CURRY

Serves 6

This simple eggplant curry goes beautifully with thosai *and it's also great with steamed rice. Long, thin eggplants are best, as the skin helps to prevent the eggplant pieces from breaking up when you fry them.*

INGREDIENTS

800 g (1 lb 12 oz) long, thin light purple
   eggplants

500 ml (17 fl oz/2 cups) vegetable oil, for
   deep-frying, plus 1 tablespoon extra

250 ml (9 fl oz/1 cup) coconut milk*

125 ml (4 fl oz/½ cup) coconut cream*

2 teaspoons Bamini's roasted curry
   powder (page 195) (or store-bought
   roasted curry powder)

1 teaspoon salt

1 red onion*, thinly sliced

1 teaspoon black mustard seeds

½ teaspoon fennel seeds

½ teaspoon cumin seeds

1 sprig curry leaves, leaves picked
   and torn

juice of 1 lime

METHOD

Cut the eggplants into quarters lengthways and then slice into 3 cm (1¼ inch) pieces. Heat the oil in a small wok over medium–high heat to approximately 180°C (350°F) (a cube of bread dropped into the oil will brown in 15 seconds). Working in five or six batches, deep-fry the eggplant pieces for 4–5 minutes, or until dark golden brown. Remove with a slotted spoon and drain on paper towel.

Drain off the oil left in the wok, wipe the wok clean with paper towel and return to a medium heat. Pour in the coconut milk and coconut cream, then stir in the curry powder and salt. Bring to just below the boil, reduce the heat and simmer for 5 minutes. Remove from the heat and set aside.

In a clay pot or heavy-based saucepan, heat the extra oil over low–medium heat and fry the onion for 3–4 minutes, or until golden brown. Add the mustard seeds, fennel seeds, cumin seeds and curry leaves and cook for 1 minute. Add the fried eggplant, coconut milk mixture and 2 tablespoons water and gently mix. Reduce the heat and simmer for 5 minutes, or until the sauce thickens and has reduced a little. Remove from the heat and add the lime juice. Rest for 10 minutes before serving. Serve warm with thosai (page 228) and green coconut chutney (page 213) and a generous sprinkle of thosai podi (page 232).

HUNGRY FOR CHANGE
Father Damian

I awake to the humming of the ceiling fan working overtime and the sound of children laughing. The sun has only just risen but the children of Point Pedro have been awake for hours.

I have come to Point Pedro to visit Anjali Aham, a counselling centre, school and youth drop-in centre, run by a local Tamil Catholic priest. I make my way downstairs and find children dancing, singing and playing games. When Father Damian walks in they all rush over to him, asking the same question: 'Hello Father, what do we have today?'

Today is a special day at Anjali Aham; it's Saturday and a free lunch is being prepared for the children. The reassurance of knowing they will receive a meal today is cause for great excitement.

A team of local women arrives laden with massive cooking pots and baskets brimming with fresh produce. The food has been purchased at the local market from funds donated by the MJF Charitable Foundation, who sponsor the weekly lunch at Anjali Aham. The children are keen to lend a hand and rush over, all trying to guess what's for lunch. Today it is *kanji*, a sweet rice porridge made from red rice, green gram, coconut milk and a mixture of seven nourishing leafy greens.

In no time, woven mats are rolled out under the mango tree in the front garden and the women set to work preparing the food. Sandradevi, the oldest woman of the group, is clearly in charge and while she attends to lighting the fire, the younger women start chopping the mountain of leafy greens. Despite the volume of food they are preparing (enough to feed 270 hungry kids), the women make it look effortless, chatting and laughing as they prepare and cook lunch.

When I first heard about Anjali Aham, I was surprised such a place existed, because there are so many things the people of northern Sri Lanka need but are living without. But the acute need for a counselling centre to address the trauma and grief from the war and the tsunami is undeniable. The centre was established in 2006 by the Missionary Oblates of Mary Immaculate (OMI Jaffna), and is run by Father Damian, a kind-hearted, introspective man who has dedicated his life to helping others.

Over our breakfast of fresh jackfruit and *pittu*, Father Damian explains how social stigma and gossip are a big problem in the community. 'Many of these women have lost their husbands in the war and have never had to work outside the family

235

home. This carries great shame for them, but they are now compelled to work to feed their children. Gossip can be very damaging and we are trying to change some of these attitudes.'

Father Damian and a team of eight counsellors and five teachers are working with the local widowed women and orphaned children to help overcome these stigmas and assist them in becoming self-sufficient. 'I want to be here and work with the families,' he explains. 'The real work is just beginning, so much needs to be done.'

Sundays are what Father Damian looks forward to most and his face lights up when he tells me about the creative arts programme for the children, which features activities such as dancing, singing, music and painting. 'This is what it's all about for me … it gives me relief from the devastation.'

The lunch being prepared today is something the whole community looks forward to and everyone is keen to pitch in. As the final ingredients are added to the *kanji*, the older children set to work washing the bowls and seating the younger children.

A group of young women arrives, who I recognise as the children's teachers; they have come on their day off to help serve the food. When it is time to eat, the women insist I eat first with the younger children. Knowing this is a customary honour, I accept their offer and take a seat. Silence soon descends; all I can hear is the sound of spoons hurriedly scraping bowls. The *kanji* is warm, creamy and sweet, and nourishing at the same time.

'The lunch being prepared today is something the whole community looks forward to and everyone is keen to pitch in.'

With lunch over, the children head out to the streets to play and I stay to chat with the teachers. Jasintha, who is more confident in English, fires off a list of questions that I have become accustomed to during my travels: 'How many children do you have? Are you married? I don't understand. Why not? And at your age? You need a good Sri Lankan husband! My aunty has a son who is looking for a foreign wife …'

Father Damian notices I'm being grilled by the women and ushers me inside. We sit at the kitchen table indulging in freshly picked mangoes. He tells me that Anjali Aham means 'offering service to God and to the people'. 'But this isn't about religion,' he is quick to add. 'There is too much to be done here to be concerned about who follows what faith.'

Most of the women and children who attend Anjali Aham are Hindu, and Father Damian respects this. I am hardly surprised when I learn that his closest friend is the local Hindu *kovil* priest and last week two chief Buddhist monks from Colombo came to stay with him.

United by a common purpose, it seems everyone in Point Pedro is working together to help rebuild the community and move on.

POINT PEDRO KANJI

Serves 6

A type of rice porridge, kanji *is a staple throughout Sri Lanka. It is creamy and sweet, made with nourishing leafy greens and served warm. Sri Lankans like their* kanji *super sweet but this recipe has less sugar than is traditionally used.*

INGREDIENTS

55 g (2 oz/¼ cup) green gram* (dried mung beans), soaked in water overnight

210 g (7½ oz/1 cup) red rice*

50 g (1¾ oz/1 cup) finely chopped leafy green vegetables, such as gotu kola*, drumstick leaves* and English spinach (use a mixture of 2 or 3)

¼ teaspoon salt

220 g (7¾ oz/1 cup) sugar

125 ml (4 fl oz/½ cup) full-cream milk

250 ml (9 fl oz/1 cup) coconut cream*

METHOD

Bring 1.25 litres (44 fl oz/5 cups) water to the boil in a large saucepan. Meanwhile, drain the soaked green gram. Wash the red rice, then combine with the green gram; wash again and drain. Add the rice and green gram to the boiling water (make sure the water comes about 3 cm (1¼ inches) above the rice). Return to the boil, then cover and simmer over low–medium heat for 15–20 minutes.

When the rice is cooked (it should be soft and slushy; add more boiling water if needed), stir in the leafy greens and salt and simmer, uncovered, for 1 minute. Stir in the sugar and simmer for a further 3 minutes, then add the milk and coconut cream and stir well to combine. Simmer over low heat for a further 5 minutes. Remove from the heat and allow to stand for 5 minutes before serving.

TAMIL COMFORT FOOD
Vigneshwaran & Malathi

The sun is just starting to rise as we leave Jaffna town and drive across a long narrow causeway to the island of Kayts. From here we will join another causeway that will take us to Punkudutivu Island. The surrounding water is a maze of fish traps, gliding wooden canoes and fishermen wading chest-deep in the water, retrieving the night's catch. The effect is hypnotic and even the spirals of razor-sharp barbed wire poking up from the water don't break my trance.

As we drive onto Kayts, the water is replaced by flat, dry grasslands and windswept palmyra palms. We pass a number of bombed-out, abandoned houses and stop at a sandstone villa overrun by vines and tree roots. The front door is missing, but the stone archway entrance invites me in. Inside are reminders of a life from long ago: a rusty wrought-iron bed frame, a bent metal chair and a collection of large blackened cooking pots.

From here we continue on, driving past colourful Hindu *kovils* (temples) and grand Catholic churches that look more like cathedrals. Some of the churches such as Saint Mary's, which was built during the British occupation, are still in use. Today a few boys are playing soccer out the front. It's hard to believe that not that long ago, during the civil war, people sought refuge here in dug-out bunkers.

When we arrive at the entrance to Punkudutivu, we are briefly stopped at a military checkpoint. Thankfully we drive through without any fuss, passing more destroyed houses. Some are missing roofs, while others have only a wall left standing or a front gate. The scene is desolate but beautiful at the same time.

We stop at the Sri Raja Rajeswari Amman Kovil, hoping to find something for breakfast. It is the first day of their Amman Pooja Festival. In front of the temple is a row of three makeshift huts erected out of woven palmyra palms. The entrance to each is adorned with bags of popcorn, spicy snacks and bunches of bananas. I enter the middle hut and am surprised to find it decorated with antique furniture. There is a carved wooden coffee table, a worn church pew and a wooden cabinet filled with interestingly shaped savoury pastries. In the corner is a plumpish woman, frying *vadai* over a fire in a big metal drum. She has a warm and inviting smile and greets me with '*vanakkam*', meaning 'hello, welcome' in Tamil.

Within seconds she brings over a plate of piping-hot *vadai*. I eagerly take one and bite into it; the crunchy exterior gives way to a soft and steamy blend of dhal, fennel seeds, curry leaves and chilli. Eaten with a cup of steaming milky tea they

quickly become addictive. Realising I can't leave without the recipe, I start hovering around where the food is being prepared.

In no time at all, I am put to work, flattening balls of *vadai* mixture into discs and plunging them into woks of hot oil. While cooking, I learn that the couple who run the stall, Vigneshwaran and his wife Malathi, have been selling food at the annual festival for the last six years. However, the set-up is only temporary and at the end of the fifteen-day festival they will dismantle their hut. I am surprised when they tell me that they both work as labourers.

> '*Within seconds she brings over a plate of piping-hot* vadai. *I eagerly take one and bite into it; the crunchy exterior gives way to a soft and steamy blend of dhal, fennel seeds, curry leaves and chilli. Eaten with a cup of steaming milky tea they quickly become addictive.*'

Malathi explains, 'We both have to work; we have three girls and need to get dowries for them.' They are especially worried about their eldest daughter, Saraniya, who is twenty, as there are very few young men left on Punkudutivu since the war. 'Saraniya is staying with my sister in Batticaloa. We are looking for a husband for her there.'

When I have exhausted all the *vadai* mixture, we start on the patties. Patties are a fried savoury pastry filled with curried potato, similar to a samosa. Malathi begins frying the cabbage and onions, adding fennel seeds, rampe, curry leaves and roasted chilli powder. When the curry leaves start to pop, releasing a peppery, slightly citrusy aroma, she adds the mashed potatoes.

Meanwhile, Vigneshwaran rolls out the dough for the patties using a soft-drink bottle. Taking a stainless-steel cup, he cuts out small circles from the dough, then spoons the curried potato into the middle of each and folds it over to form a half-moon shape. Like most snacks in Sri Lanka, they are deep-fried, resulting in a golden puffy pastry. This is comfort food at its best.

Over a plate of patties, Malathi tells me how she is hopeful about her family's future here on Punkudutivu and is certain more families will return as the island is slowly rebuilt.

PARUPPU VADAI

Makes 18–20

Vadai is a savoury snack, or 'short eat' as Sri Lankans call them, made from deep-fried pulses. There is paruppu vadai made from chana dhal and ulundu vadai made from black gram. Malathi made her vadai from chana dhal; they were incredibly moreish, especially when accompanied with a cup of hot, sweet milky tea.

INGREDIENTS

400 g (14 oz/2 cups) chana dhal*, soaked in water for 4 hours

1 red onion*, finely chopped

4 cloves garlic, ground into a paste

4 dried long red chillies*, stalks removed and chopped

½ long green chilli*, finely chopped

1 sprig curry leaves, leaves picked and finely chopped

1 teaspoon fennel seeds

1 teaspoon cumin seeds

1½ teaspoons salt

about 1 tablespoon plain flour (optional)

vegetable oil, for deep-frying

METHOD

Drain the soaked dhal, then rinse and drain again thoroughly. Using a food processor, process the dhal into a coarse paste (without adding any water). Transfer to a large bowl and set aside.

Pulse the chopped onion in the processor for a few seconds, then transfer to a small bowl and add the garlic paste, dried chillies, green chilli, curry leaves, fennel seeds, cumin seeds and salt; mix to combine. Add the onion mixture to the dhal paste and mix well with your hands (you don't need to add any water, as the water released from the onions will be enough). If needed, add a little flour to bring all the ingredients together.

Take 1 tablespoon of the mixture in the palm of your hand and shape it into a ball the size of a lime, then flatten between the palms of your hands to form a disc approximately 6 cm (2½ inches) in diameter and 1 cm (½ inch) thick. Repeat with the remaining mixture.

Fill a wok one-third full of oil and heat to approximately 160°C (315°F) (a cube of bread dropped into the oil will brown in 30 seconds). Working in batches, deep-fry the vadai for 4–5 minutes, or until golden brown and crisp. Drain on paper towel and serve hot.

VEGETABLE PATTIES

Makes 32

Sri Lankan patties are unlike the ones I'm used to; these are deep-fried pastry parcels filled with curried vegetables, similar to a samosa. Vigneshwaran wrapped up a few patties for me to eat on the drive back to Jaffna, but we only made it down the road before they were all gone.

FILLING

1 tablespoon coconut oil*
200 g (7 oz) cabbage, thinly sliced
4 dried long red chillies*, chopped
6 small pink Asian shallots*, finely chopped
1 teaspoon fennel seeds
1 teaspoon roasted chilli powder*
½ teaspoon ground turmeric
1 sprig curry leaves, leaves picked
   and roughly chopped
6 cm (2½ inch) piece rampe (pandanus)
   leaf*, chopped
1 teaspoon salt, dissolved in 1 tablespoon
   warm water

1 kg (2 lb 4 oz) potatoes, boiled, peeled
   and mashed
vegetable oil, for deep-frying

DOUGH

600 g (1 lb 5 oz/4 cups) plain flour
1 teaspoon bicarbonate of soda
1 teaspoon salt
1 tablespoon coconut oil*, plus
   2 tablespoons extra
250 ml (9 fl oz/1 cup) full-cream milk

METHOD

To make the filling, heat the coconut oil in a wok or deep frying pan over medium heat. Add the cabbage, dried chillies, shallots, fennel seeds, chilli powder, turmeric, curry leaves and rampe; cook for 5 minutes, or until the shallots are golden brown. Add the salty water and remove from the heat. Stir in the mashed potato until well combined. Set aside to cool to room temperature.

To make the dough, sift the flour, bicarbonate of soda and salt into a bowl. Using your hands, mix in the coconut oil, then gradually add the milk, about 2 tablespoons at a time. Continue to work the dough until it is soft and pliable; you may need to add a little water (up to 4 tablespoons). Shape the dough into a large ball and rub with a little extra coconut oil.

Roll out half the dough on a lightly floured surface to 3 mm (⅛ inch) thick. Cut out 10 cm (4 inch) circles with a pastry cutter or glass. Spoon a heaped tablespoon of the filling into the centre of each circle and fold in half. Use your fingers to press the edges together, brushing the edge of the dough with a little water if necessary. Re-roll the offcuts and use as well. Repeat with the remaining dough.

Fill a wok one-third full of oil and heat to approximately 180°C (350°F) (a cube of bread dropped into the oil will brown in 15 seconds). Deep-fry the patties in batches for 2–3 minutes until crisp and golden, turning them over halfway through cooking time. Remove with a slotted spoon and drain on paper towel. Serve hot or cold.

VEGETABLE ROTI ROLLS

Makes about 15

Another popular snack or 'short eat', roti rolls are made from paper-thin pieces of dough, which are filled with curried vegetables or meat, then folded into a triangle or shaped like a spring roll. They are sometimes crumbed and deep-fried. Vigneshwaran and Malathi filled their vegetable roti with a potato and cabbage curry and fried them on a cast-iron plate over an open fire.

FILLING
Use the same filling as vegetable patties
  (page 249)

DOUGH
900 g (2 lb/6 cups) plain flour
1½ teaspoons salt
60 ml (2 fl oz/¼ cup) coconut oil*,
  plus extra for cooking

METHOD
Prepare the filling and set it aside.

To make the dough, sift the flour and salt into a large bowl. Using your hands, mix in the coconut oil and about 8 tablespoons water, adding a tablespoon at a time. Continue to work the dough until it is smooth and elastic; you may need to add a little more water (2–4 tablespoons) and oil to get the right consistency. Divide the dough into 15 pieces and shape each piece into a ball a little smaller than a tennis ball. As you finish shaping each ball, cover it in plastic wrap so it doesn't dry out.

Take one ball of dough and roll it out on a clean work surface into a very thin rectangle, approximately 28 x 30 cm (11¼ x 12 inches). With the longest sides at the top and bottom, place 2 heaped tablespoons of the filling along the length of the dough, about a third of the way up from the bottom. Fold in the two short sides and then tightly roll it up like a spring roll.

Heat a flat griddle or cast-iron frying pan over medium heat and brush it lightly with coconut oil. Fry the rolls for 4–5 minutes, turning them over every minute or so until each side is golden brown. Stand them up on each end as well, to cook the edges. Serve hot or cold.

GLOSSARY

All of the following ingredients are available from Indian and Sri Lankan specialty stores, unless specified. The ingredients included in this glossary are marked with an asterix * in the recipes.

Ajinomoto

A powdered food seasoning often used in Asian cooking to enhance flavour. Ajinomoto is the trade name for monosodium glutamate (MSG). Available from Asian grocers.

Asian shallots, pink

See Onions

Basil seeds

Tiny black seeds from the basil plant, which swell and develop a glutinous coating when soaked. Added to drinks and desserts. Available from Asian grocers and specialist spice stores.

Bitter gourd

Also known as bitter melon. These look similar to a large cucumber with ridged, bumpy skin. The Sri Lankan variety has quite pronounced teeth-like bumps on the skin and is a darker green than the Asian variety, which is more readily available. They are extremely bitter; blanching them in boiling water helps reduce the bitterness.

Black gram

Black gram are dried black mung beans, known as *ulundu* in Tamil and *urad dhal* in Hindi. They have a thick black skin and are creamy white inside. Sold whole, skinned or split. Used to make a fermented batter for *idli* and *thosai*.

Black gram flour: Made from ground whole black gram. You can buy it roasted or unroasted, or make your own.

To make roasted black gram flour:
Wash and dry the whole black gram, then dry-roast in a heavy-based frying pan or wok over low heat for 4 minutes. Cool slightly, then using a mortar and pestle (or spice grinder), pound the black gram into a fine powder.

Chana dhal

Made from split skinned black chickpeas, chana dhal looks very similar to yellow split peas. You can use yellow split peas instead, but they don't hold their shape as well.

Chilli powder

Made from ground dried long red chillies. Both roasted and unroasted chilli powders are available, so be careful to buy the right one. Unroasted chilli powder is bright red in colour, whereas roasted chilli powder is dark browny red and adds a slightly different flavour and colour to dishes.

Chillies, dried

Dried long red chillies: Sun-dried whole long red chillies.
Chilli pieces: Finely chopped, dried long red chillies, similar to chilli flakes.

Chillies, fresh

This book calls for three types of fresh chillies:

Thin green chillies: A thin, knobbly light green chilli, available from Sri Lankan and Indian stores. They are very hot, so you may prefer to adjust the quantities specified in the recipes. Alternatively you can use small green chillies from your supermarket.

Medium green chillies: Light green chillies with a smooth skin. They are plumper but smaller in length than thin green chillies and not as hot. Used for making curd chillies.

Long green chillies: Darker in colour and the mildest of the three chillies. You can find these at your local supermarket.

Coconut, freshly scraped

Use hard, brown-shelled coconuts. When buying a fresh coconut, shake it first to check there is a good amount of water in it.

To crack a coconut in half: Trim off any thick husk fibres. Hold the coconut in the palm of your hand over a large bowl (to catch the water when the coconut splits). Note the three seams that run along the coconut (they look like thick veins). First use the blunt edge of a heavy cleaver and tap firmly along each seam (without cracking them) while rotating the coconut in the palm of your hand. Then turn the coconut so the three eyes face your thumb. Using the sharp edge of the cleaver, whack hard around its equator until the coconut splits open. If necessary, use the tip of the blade to prise open the two halves.

To scrape out the coconut flesh: Securely attach a coconut scraper to the work bench and place a bowl under the bladed spindle to catch the coconut scrapings. Hold the coconut half over the spindle and use your other hand to turn the handle. Turn the coconut until all the white flesh has been grated (be careful not to grate into the brown skin lining the shell).

NOTE: 1 medium coconut will yield approximately 250 g (9 oz) scraped coconut.

Coconut cream & coconut milk

The liquid inside the coconut is known as coconut water or juice, and not coconut milk, as is sometimes thought.

Coconut milk (and coconut cream) is the liquid extracted from the grated coconut flesh. In Sri Lanka, coconut cream is known as the 'first extract' or 'thick coconut milk', and is very thick and creamy. Coconut milk is the 'second extract' and is much thinner.

To make coconut cream (first extract): Place the freshly scraped coconut from one coconut in a large bowl and add 185 ml (6 fl oz/¾ cup) cold water (or coconut water) and stir to combine. Take a handful of the coconut scrapings and squeeze hard, releasing the liquid back into the bowl. Return the squeezed coconut scrapings back to the bowl and stir to combine. Repeat the process until you have extracted about 125 ml (4 fl oz/½ cup) of thick and creamy liquid (coconut cream). Strain through a fine sieve into another bowl and set aside. Empty the contents of the sieve back into the first bowl so you can re-use the scrapings to extract the coconut milk.

To make coconut milk (second extract): Add about 310 ml (10¾ fl oz/1¼ cups) water to the squeezed coconut scrapings and repeat the above process until you have about 375 ml (13 fl oz/1½ cups) of thin coconut milk. Strain through a fine sieve.

Tinned & powdered: Making your own coconut cream and milk helps to achieve an authentic Sri Lankan flavour and these are not as rich as the tinned or powdered varieties. Most people won't have the time to make their own, so I've tried to use quantities based on tin size where possible. The thickness and consistency can vary depending on the brand you use, so you may need to adjust the quantities accordingly. I prefer to use the Kara brand, as it's really thick and I find it doesn't split as easily when heated.

If you want to use powdered coconut to make coconut cream, dissolve 2 tablespoons powder in 250 ml (9 fl oz/1 cup) lukewarm water. For coconut milk, dissolve 2 tablespoons powder in 500 ml (17 fl oz/2 cups) lukewarm water.

Coconut oil

Extracted from pressed coconut flesh. It can be heated to higher temperatures than vegetable oil before it reaches smoking point. It is much cheaper to buy it from Indian and Sri Lankan specialty stores rather than from health food stores, but make sure you ask for coconut oil for cooking and not the one used for your hair.

Coconut vinegar

Made from fermented coconut water (or sometimes the sap of the coconut tree). It is slightly sour and acidic, and cloudy white in colour. Available from Asian grocers. Substitute with rice vinegar.

Curd

Traditionally made from buffalo milk, which is boiled and cooled, then poured into a clay pot to set. Curd with treacle is a popular dessert in Sri Lanka. Buffalo curd is not widely available in Australia, however if you are lucky enough to find buffalo yoghurt, it's very similar. Substitute with a thick unsweetened natural yoghurt, such as Greek-style yoghurt, and make sure you choose a full-fat yoghurt for the best results.

Dried fish

Fish that has been filleted, rubbed in salt and left in the sun to dry. It has a pungent aroma, but adds a great flavour to dishes. Look for dried white fish that is thick and not too hard. If it's really hard, soak it in water for about 10 minutes before you cut it.

Drumstick leaves

Small, round green leaves with a slightly bitter taste, from the drumstick tree (or murunga tree). Remove the leaves from the thin stems before cooking. Added to curries, dhal and soups, or stir-fried and served as a side dish. Available from some Asian grocers.

Egg yellow powdered food colouring

Dissolved in water and used to enhance the colour and look of dishes. Use sparingly, as it is highly concentrated. Contains tartrazine, a synthetic yellow food dye. There has been some noted intolerance of this ingredient, with side effects such hyperactivity and asthma. Substitute with saffron or turmeric.

Flour

See Black gram flour; Odiyal flour; Red rice flour, fine; Roasted rice flour, white or red

Goroka

Also known as kokam, this is used as a souring and thickening agent in cooking. It is a small dark purple fruit with a very thick rind. The segments are dried in the sun, turning it black and hard. Goroka can be added whole to curries and removed after cooking, or soaked in hot water to soften it, the seeds removed and discarded, then ground into a paste. Available from specialist spice shops. Substitute with tamarind pulp.

Gotu kola

Also known as pennywort, this leafy green herb is a member of the parsley family and has small fan-shaped leaves and a fine stem. It is used as a medicinal herb and is highly regarded in Ayurvedic medicine. Native to Sri Lanka, it also grows in northern Queensland. It is mostly available during summer in Australia, and is sold in some Asian grocers. Substitute with flat-leaf parsley.

Green gram

Also known as dried mung beans or moong dhal, these are small dried green beans with a creamy yellow inside. Mild in flavour and used in savoury and sweet dishes. The recipes in this book call for whole green gram, although they are also available skinned and split.

Jackfruit, young green
See Polos

Jaggery & jaggery powder
An unrefined palm sugar made by boiling the sap from palm trees. Kithul palm jaggery is the sweetest and most prized, with coconut palm jaggery and palmyra palm jaggery being more common. Sold in blocks, which can be grated or chopped into pieces, and in powdered form, which looks similar to brown sugar. Jaggery varies in colour from light golden to dark brown and has a rich, caramel flavour. Available from Asian grocers and some supermarkets. Substitute with soft brown sugar.

Kanda leaf
Used to wrap and steam food in, and serve food on. The leaves are bright green with fine veins. Substitute with banana leaves.

Maldive fish
An essential ingredient in Sri Lankan cooking, Maldive fish is the key ingredient in *seeni sambol* and adds an authentic Sri Lankan flavour. Made from skipjack tuna that has been boiled, smoked and sun-dried, giving it a salty, subtle smoky flavour and a strong aroma. Sold as chips, pieces or flakes, but try to buy the flakes, as they are easier to pound using a mortar and pestle. The chips are harder and need to be processed in a spice grinder or small food processor. Substitute with ground dried sprats or dried shrimp.

Manioc
Also known as cassava, this is a long tuberous starchy root vegetable with brown fibrous skin and white flesh. The thick skin needs to be removed before cooking. Frozen manioc is more readily available; these are already peeled. Both fresh and frozen manioc are available from Asian grocers.

Odiyal flour
Also known as palmyra flour, odiyal flour is made from the ground dried roots of a young palmyra palm. The dried roots are also eaten as a snack. Used mainly in Jaffna cuisine for thickening *odiyal kool* (seafood soup). This starchy flour has a bitter taste.

Onions
Small pink Asian shallots: These are the size of garlic cloves, pinky purple in colour and have a mild, sweet flavour. Don't confuse them with French shallots (eschalots), which are golden in colour and much larger.

Red onions: The red onions used in Sri Lankan cooking are slightly different from the red Spanish onions commonly sold in most supermarkets; they are smaller and paler in colour with a slightly milder flavour. Available from Asian grocers.

Polos
Young jackfruit that have not yet ripened. Polos are smaller in size than jackfruit and need longer cooking time. Available from Asian grocers, but you may need to pre-order them: ask for unripe baby jackfruit, as polos is the Sinhala word. If unavailable, tinned is a great alternative.

Rampe leaf
Also known as pandanus, pandan leaf or screwpine leaf, these long, dark green leaves have a lovely subtle fragrance and are used for flavouring both sweet and savoury dishes. The fresh leaves are sold in bunches from Asian grocers.

Rasavalli
A purple yam that grows on the Jaffna Peninsula. Frozen rasavalli is available from selected Sri Lankan specialty stores; these are already peeled. Substitute with fresh Asian purple yam.

Red rice flour, fine

Made from ground red rice. If purchasing fine red rice flour (for making *mothagam* or *konda kavum*), buy 'string hopper red rice flour'; it has a similar consistency to cornflour.

Rice

Red rice: Has a nutty flavour, is high in fibre and contains less starch than white rice, and takes longer to cook. Usually sold unpolished with a little of the husk left on. There are many different types of red rice and it can be confusing which one to buy. Most of the recipes in this book call for medium-grain red rice, called 'raw red rice' (don't mistake it for red basmati rice). If you are making *kanji* or *kola kenda*, buy a raw red rice with less husk, as the rice breaks up more easily.

Samba rice: A tiny short-grain, oval-shaped rice grown in Sri Lanka. It has a distinct taste and a pungent aroma. You can buy white or red samba rice.

Roasted rice flour, white or red

Made from ground white or red rice, which has been dry-roasted. It has a slightly stronger flavour and aroma, and is darker in colour than unroasted rice flour. Commonly used for making *pittu*.

Seviyan vermicelli noodles, dried

Thin, dried vermicelli noodles made from semolina and broken into small 1.5 cm (⅝ inch) pieces. Used to make a variety of Tamil desserts.

Snake beans

Thin, very long, dark green beans, also known as Chinese long beans. Sold in bunches, they are available from Asian grocers.

Sprats

Whole dried baby fish, usually anchovies. They are salty and pungent, but add a great flavour to dishes. Try to buy dried sprats that have had the heads removed. Available from Asian grocers.

Tamarind pulp

Tamarind pulp comes from inside the pod of a tamarind plant and is used as a souring agent. You can buy it as a ready-made purée (concentrate), but I prefer to buy the block of pulp that still contains the seeds; this needs to be soaked and strained to make tamarind water. Available from Asian grocers.

To make tamarind water: Soak the tamarind pulp in warm water for 10 minutes. Strain through a sieve over a bowl and use the back of a spoon to press the tamarind through the sieve, extracting as much of the pulp as possible. Scrape off any pulp from underneath the sieve and add to the bowl of water. Discard the fibres and seeds left in the sieve.

Treacle

Sri Lankan treacle is made from the coconut or kithul palm. It is a thick, dark syrup used as a sweetener, similar to maple syrup.

COOKING EQUIPMENT

Clay pot
Called a *chatty* in Tamil and *hattiya* in Sinhala, these deep clay pots are used to cook directly on an open fire or gas stove, and add a great flavour to dishes. Available from Sri Lankan specialty stores. A new clay pot needs to be seasoned before use: soak it in cold water overnight before you first start cooking with it. Substitute with a cast-iron or heavy-based saucepan.

Coconut scraper
There are two types of coconut scrapers used in Sri Lanka: the traditional oval metal spike attached to a low stool; and the more commonly used metal-bladed spindle, which looks like a citrus juicer. This is clamped to a work bench and operated with a handle. I wish I had discovered them years ago, as they are really easy to use.

Idli steamer
A stainless-steel or aluminium pot with a tight-fitting lid, housing two or three *idli* trays, which have round indentations for the batter (similar to egg poachers).

Kokis mould
A metal mould, usually the shape of a wheel, attached to a thin metal rod with a wooden handle. These are used to make a thin, crisp deep-fried biscuit called *kokis*. Available from Sri Lankan specialty stores.

Pittu steamer
There are two types of *pittu* steamers used in Sri Lanka. In Jaffna they use a conical-shaped basket made out of woven palmyra leaves; the other, more common, variety is a stainless-steel or bamboo cylinder. These are then placed inside a tall narrow steamer.

Small wok
I bought a small wok from a Sri Lankan and Indian specialty store, which I find incredibly useful. It has a flat bottom (about 10 cm (4 inches) in diameter) with 7 cm (2¾ inch) high sides (not to be confused with a hopper pan, which is a bit smaller and has a rounded bottom). It's perfect for frying, dry-roasting, tempering and also cooking side curries.

Spice grinders
There are two main spice grinders used in Sri Lanka: a heavy stone base with a stone rolling pin; and a massive wooden mortar and pestle. I find an average-sized sturdy mortar and pestle is usually sufficient, and I like to use a spice grinder for spices that are too hard to grind in the mortar. I also like to use the spice grinder for ingredients such as Maldive fish, sprats and green gram.

Roti pan
Known as a *tava* in Tamil and *thatiya* in Sinhala, this flat cast-iron griddle is used for making *roti* and *thosai*. A shallow cast-iron frying pan is a good alternative.

Wok
I like to use a large wok with two metal handles, similar to the woks used in Asian cooking. *Thaachchiya* is the Sinhala word for wok and *thaachchi* is the Tamil word.

ALTERNATIVE NAMES

baking paper	baking parchment	rampe	pandanus leaf, screwpine
bicarbonate of soda	baking soda		
biscuits	cookies	roma tomato	plum tomato
caster sugar	superfine sugar	snake beans	Chinese long beans, yard-long beans
coriander leaves	cilantro leaves		
eggplant	aubergine		
flat-leaf parsley	Italian parsley	stock cubes	bouillon cubes
full-cream milk	whole milk	sugar	white granulated sugar
jaggery	palm sugar		
muslin	cheesecloth	tomato purée	tomato passata, puréed tomatoes
moreton bay/balmain bug	flat-head lobster		
plain flour	all-purpose flour	treacle	maple syrup or golden syrup
pumpkin	winter squash		
pumpkin, Jap	kent pumpkin	yeast, dried	powdered yeast
prawns	shrimp		

A NOTE ON THE MEASUREMENTS

This book uses Australian metric measurements.
1 cup = 250 ml (9 fl oz)
1 teaspoon = 5 ml
1 tablespoon = 20 ml

A US cup = 235 ml (8 fl oz). If you are using an American cup,
please add an extra tablespoon to your ingredients.

A US/UK tablespoon = 15 ml (½ fl oz). If you are using a US/UK tablespoon, for most
recipes the difference is negligible. However, to be accurate you may want to add an
extra teaspoon of the ingredient for each tablespoon listed.

For US readers, 115 g (4 oz/½ cup) = 1 stick of butter

INDEX

*Page numbers in **bold** indicate a recipe.

Bohoma isthuthi / Thank you / Mikka nandri

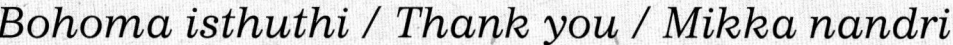

First and foremost, I would like to thank Merrill J. Fernando, his sons Dilhan and Malik, and Dilmah for sponsoring the book. Thank you for offering me this wonderful opportunity. I am especially grateful to Dilhan C. Fernando for trusting that I could capture the essence of Sri Lanka and for giving me the freedom to do so. Also, the Dilmah Brand Marketing Team, for seeing the potential for my book and your kind assistance.

Thank you to the MJF Charitable Foundation for its support, especially for connecting me with some of the participants in their programmes. I hope this book inspires others to find out more about the Foundation's remarkable work: http://www.mjffoundation.org/. I also thank Dilmah Conservation.

A special thank you to Neyome Sathyaseelan for accompanying me on my travels and showing me a side of Sri Lanka I didn't know existed. I could not have written and photographed this book without you.

A heartfelt thank you to the people of Sri Lanka who opened their homes, kitchens and hearts to me, generously sharing their stories and recipes. My hardest task was culling all your stories and recipes to fit in this book.

Thank you to my designer Hugh Ford, for turning my photographs and words into a stunning book. Publishing a book was a new experience for me and you were always there to answer any of my questions and made me feel part of the design process. Thanks for showing Murdoch my book — you are the world's best agent! Thank you to my encouraging and patient editor, Kim Rowney; you embraced this book so wholeheartedly, I felt like you travelled to Sri Lanka with me. Sonia Greig, thank you for your enthusiasm and hard work testing the recipes. You went to incredible lengths to make each recipe perfect, including painstakingly peeling the black gram!

Being approached by Murdoch Books to publish my first book was beyond my wildest dreams. A special thanks to Robert Gorman, Sue Hines, Diana Hill and Claire Grady.

Although most of the photos were taken in Sri Lanka, I would like to thank Michelle Noerianto for your beautiful styling of the dishes shot in the studio. Thank you also to Sonia Greig and Peta Dent for cooking at the photo shoot. And to Spiceland in Sydney, for guiding me through the maze of Sri Lankan ingredients and for your helpful recipe tips.

A special thank you to Alan Benson for your never-ending support and for generously sharing your time, expertise and friendship with me. I feel privileged to have been mentored by a photographer as gifted as yourself.

Thank you to my friends for all your support, especially Amanda; you have always encouraged me to follow my passion and take risks. Finally, I would like to thank my family, especially my sister, Anna, for your encouragement and support. Thanks for letting me take over the kitchen with my jumble of pots, spices and boxes of ingredients; and for your patience with me while I was completely consumed with this project!

Published in 2013 by Murdoch Books. Reprined 2017
in association with Ceylon Tea Services PLC

Murdoch Books Australia
83 Alexander St
Crows Nest, NSW 2065
AUSTRALIA
Phone: +61 (0) 2 8425 0100
Fax: +61 (0) 2 9906 2218
www.murdochbooks.com.au
info@murdochbooks.com.au

Murdoch Books UK
Ormond House
26–27 Boswell Street
London WC1N 3JZ
Phone: +44 (0) 20 8785 5995
murdochbooks.co.uk
info@murdochbooks.co.uk

Ceylon Tea Services PLC
MJF Holdings
111 Negombo Road
Peliyagoda
Sri Lanka
Phone: +94 11 482 2000
Fax: + 94 11 482 2001
www.dilmah.com

Photographer: Bree Hutchins
Concept and design: Hugh Ford Design
Editor: Kim Rowney
Recipe testing: Sonia Greig
Food stylists: Michelle Noerianto, pp. 41, 51, 78, 101, 109, 123, 130, 152, 155, 161, 162, 167, 181, 203, 204, 208, 229; Anna Hutchins, pp. 52, 81, 128.

A cataloguing-in-publication entry is available from the catalogue of the National Library of Australia at www.nla.gov.au.

A catalogue record for this book is available from the British Library.

Colour reproduction by Splitting Image, Clayton, Victoria.

Printed by 1010 Printing International Limited, China.

AUTHOR'S NOTE: As I do not speak Sinhala or Tamil, I apologise if any errors have arisen when information was translated to me, and also for any errors in relation to historical facts or cultural customs and practices. To the best of my ability, I endeavoured to have these checked.

"
යුරෝපීය ජාතීන්ගේ
මංකොල්ලකාරී
ආක්‍රමණික රටාව තුළ
සුදු මිනිසා හැරුණු විට
අන් සියලු දෙනා
තිරිසනුන් සේ සිතමින්
කටයුතු කරමින් මෙම
ආක්‍රමණික කාල
පරිච්ඡේදය දියත් විය.

සිංහලය යුරෝපා
ජාතීන්ගේ දඩබිමක් බවට
පත් වන්නේ මේ
ආකාරයෙන් ඔවුන්
කටයුතු කරන සමයේය.

මෙම තත්ත්වය තුළ
පැවැති සිංහල
ශිෂ්ටාචාරය නරුම
වෙනසකට භාජනය
කරන ලද අතර, පැවැති
රාජ්‍යයේ සියලුම අංග
පරිණාමයකින් තොරව
බලහත්කාරයෙන්
වෙනස්කම් සඳහා
භාජනය කරනු ලැබීය.

සැකවින් කිවහොත් රටේ
භෞතික පිහිටීම හැරුණු
විට අන් සියලු දේ
යුරෝපීය
ආක්‍රමණිකයාගේ
කැමැත්ත අනුව වෙනස්

ගන්නට යන විට එදා යටත් විජිත ඇති කළ පිරිසම
මානව හිමිකම් පෑදී දැ සමග පටලවාගෙන එයින්
ගැලවෙනවා වෙනුවට නව ප්‍රශ්න රටට ඇති කරමින්
තිබේ.

යටත්විජිතකරණයට පෙර සංවෘත කෘෂි ආර්ථික
රටාව තුළ ණය බර එකී රටකට දැරිය නොහැකි
මට්ටමේ ... ශ්‍රී ලංකාව බ ... වශයෙන් සැකසී
... ජනතාවගේ ජීවන තත්ත්වය මූලික ... සමය.
තිබුණේ ... ක්‍රම පටිපාටිය යටත්විජිතවාදීන් එදා
වැඩිදියුණු ... ආර්ථිකය කරා රට බිඳ වැටී ගියේ අතර 1977
තිබූ සමෝධානික ජීවන තත්ත්වය බිඳවැටී මොඩලයත් සමග
දී ඇතිකරන ලද විවෘත ආර්ථික මොඩලයුනි. මේ
ණය බරින් පිඩිත දේශයක් බවට පත්විම ඇරැඹුණි. එය
සඳහා යටත් විජිතකරණය පමණක් නොව
අන්ධානුකරණයෙන් පිළිගත් පාලක පන්තියටද
වගකීමක් පැවරේ. නමුත් ලෝකයටම එයින් පිළි
තිබෙන ආර්ථික මොඩලයක් හේතුවෙන් පත් විසඳ
... නොහැකි තැනකට ශ්‍රී ලංකාවද ලෙස
තිබේ. යටත් විජිතකරණය, ගෝලීයකරණය එයට
අර්ගහන්ව වෙස් මාරුකර ගැනීම සමග ප්‍රශ්න
හසුවීමේ ප්‍රතිඵලයක් ලෙස යටත්විජිත සමයේ
නව ආකාරයකින් ශ්‍රී ලාංකේය සමාජයේ මතුවී තිබේ.

ඉදිරි පරම්පරා ගණනාවක්ම එතෙරට ණය ගෙවීම
සඳහා යොමුවී තිබෙන්නේ මෙම ක්‍රියාවලියේ පිටුබලය
ඇතිව.

යටත්විජිතකරණයෙන් නිදහස් වීම හෙවත් පොඩි
කුඩුකින් ලොකු කුඩුවකට ඒමට ශ්‍රී ලංකාවට 1948 දී
හැකියාව ලැබුණත් එම අවස්ථාවෙන් හෝ රට ගෙන
තිබෙන ප්‍රයෝජන අල්පය. 1970 වන
ලංකාවේ පරම අධිකරණ බලය තිබුණේ එංගලන්තයේ
ප්‍රිවි කවුන්සිලයේ සතුවය. 1970 ජනරජ ආණ්ඩුක්‍රම
මගින් ඒ සඳහා ප්‍රතිකර්ම කරන ලදි. සමහර අංශයන්හි
ඒවැනි යටත යන දෑරීම සඳහා අවකාශ තිබුණ ද ඒ සඳහා
පාලක පැලැන්තිය සෑමුවී නොතිබිනි. එල්. ටී. ටී. ඊ.
ත්‍රස්තවාදය මුල්මැසින්ම පෑදය වශයෙන් පරාජය කර
තිබෙන තත්ත්වයකදී වුවද දෙමළ වර්ගවාදයට
බෝදුන් පළාත් සභා වැනි කජ්ජම් රට විසින් තවම
කරපින්නාගෙන සිටින්නේ, 1948 සිට 1970 තෙක් ප්‍රිවි
කවුන්සිලය කරපින්නාගෙන සිටි අන්දමට. මෙවැනි
දේවල් වලින් ජාතියක් ලෙස අපට නිදහස ලැබීම
යයි තැන් තිබෙතත්, චහල් මානසිකත්වය හිමි පාලක
හා විත් පැලැන්තිය ඒ සඳහා බාධකයක් ලෙස
ක්‍රියාකර තිබේ.

රට ඒවැනි නිදහසක් අවශ්‍ය වන්නා සේම
පරිපූර්ණ නිදහසක් හිමි ජාතියක් නිර්මාණය වන්නේ
නිහල් පුද්ගලයා තැනීමෙනි. ඒ සඳහා සමාජයේ
නිහල් පුද්ගලයකු නීතියේ ආධිපත්‍ය තිබෙන
යුතු පළමු සුසකම නීතියේ ආධිපත්‍ය තිබෙන
ඉහලින් තිබීමය, වත්මනේ රට තුළ ඒ සඳහා තිබෙන
අවකාශ ජන සමාජයේ එදිනෙද කියුම් කෙරුම
වලින් තේරුම් ගත හැකිය, කැළ නීතිය රටේ මූලික
තිතිය වීම නම රට නිහල් වුවත් ඒයින් ජනතාවට
තිබෙන එළයක් නැත. නිදහස් රටක සිර ගෙවලටත්
... තිබෙන සඟතියක් නැ... වැනි